THESE THINGS ARE WRITTEN

An introduction to the religious ideas of the Bible

JAMES M. EFIRD

JOHN KNOX PRESS
ATLANTA

10 9 8 7 6 5 4 3 2

The Scripture quotations in this publication are from the Revised Standard Version
Bible, copyright 1946, 1952, and © 1971 by the Division of Christian Education,
National Council of the Churches of Christ in the U.S.A. and used by permission.

Library of Congress Cataloging in Publication Data

Efird, James M
  These things are written.

  Bibliography: p.
  1. Bible—Criticism, interpretation, etc. I. Title.
BS511.2.E33   220.6   77–15749
ISBN 0–8042–0073–4

Dedicated to
My MOTHER and FATHER
who have demonstrated through their lives
the essence of biblical religion

Acknowledgments

There are far too many persons to whom I owe great debts and who are in one way or another a significant part of this book for me to attempt to name them one by one. I simply wish to say thanks to everyone who has helped in this enterprise. There are, however, several who do deserve to be mentioned by name: my colleague and friend, Professor Donn Michael Farris, who has been a source of encouragement for many years now; to the students in my Religion 55 class at Duke University who have served without complaining as "guinea pigs" in the structuring and completion of this project; to Dr. Richard A. Ray and his fine staff at the John Knox Press for their help, assistance, and encouragement; and to my wife, Vivian, who typed the manuscript from my handwritten copy (no mean task!) and who in every way has encouraged and sustained me in good and bad times.

Durham, N. C.
August, 1977

James M. Efird

Preface

Almost every educational institution with a department of religion has a course in its curriculum in which there is a rapid survey of the religion of the Bible. In addition, many church groups have set for themselves the task of studying the "whole Bible" within a certain period of time. It is always difficult to fit the amount of material to be covered into the time allotted since there is such a vast amount of material to be covered ranging over a long period of history. But the endeavor need not be given up as totally impossible if one is selective and sticks to the main path. To accomplish this task, however, requires that some aspects of biblical research and interest be emphasized while others must temporarily be either ignored or only briefly touched. There are times and places, however, where a rapid overview of the religious teachings of the Bible serves us well. This work is intended as a source where the serious student of the Bible may in some way come to see an overview of the biblical religious teaching and development without becoming so bogged down in minutiae that the forest is missed for looking only at a tree or two! The purpose, then, of this book is to assist the person who wishes to obtain a rapid overview of the basic religious ideas and the development of these ideas which are contained within the books of the Old Testament and the New Testament.

As is well known, religion is a phenomenon of human experience which is universal. And religion has two basic aspects: (1) a subjective or personal level; and (2) an objective or cultic level. The religion of the Bible has, naturally, both aspects, but in this book the former will be the center of concentration, for it is on this thread, i.e. that of encounter and relationship with the God revealed in the biblical writings, that the fundamental religious ideas of the Bible find continuity. Therefore, we shall not emphasize cultic practices, which often change or even die out, but the personal elements of the religious experience which live on.

Further, it should be emphasized that this particular work is not designed as a substitute for a good historical-critical introduction to the Old and/or New Testament. Neither is it designed as a detailed history of those times, nor as an introduction to the various types of literature incorporated into the biblical books. There are already good works which cover these areas well. This work will make use of all these types of approaches and methodologies, and there will be points at which one or another of these types of approaches will be utilized more intensively, depending on the circumstances surrounding the material under consideration. The main purpose overall, however, will be an attempt to give a chronological developmental survey of the basic *religious* ideas and thinking in the biblical tradition.

The book is designed so that it may be used either in a classroom or study group as a basic text or as supplementary reading, or by an individual who wishes to study the Bible but has no group with which to study. In either case the book is intended to be used in the following manner. First of all, the student should read the chapters of this text. Then one should read the biblical references which are listed at the conclusion of each chapter. This is very important since the passages selected are illustrative of the points made in the chapters of the text. This information may then be supplemented by lectures, or by additional reading (also listed at the conclusion of each chapter), or both.

When one comes to the conclusion of the study project, there should have been gained an overall perspective of the development of basic biblical ideas and the foundation laid for further and more detailed study of the Old and New Testaments as one's interests may dictate.

This collection of writings which is known as the Bible, the thirty-nine books of the Old Testament and the twenty-seven of the New Testament, came into being over a period of about six hundred years (some of the sources being even older), and how these stories and ideas came together makes a fascinating study. To that study we now turn, and it is the hope of the author that the student will find much more here than simply the study of something from the past. It is hoped that something in it will speak to our present life!

Contents

1	Presuppositions for Biblical Study	13
2	Religion to the Conquest	26
3	The Religion of the Conquest and the Kingdom	37
4	The Prophetic Movement	48
5	Religious Development in the Post-Exilic Period	68
6	The Hellenistic Period and the Rise of Apocalyptic	78
7	New Testament Background and the Synoptic Gospels	89
8	The Early Church and the Career of Paul	109
9	Paul's Letters and Beliefs	121
10	The Post-Apostolic Period	139
11	The Gospel of John	154
12	Conclusion	163
Bibliography		168

1
Presuppositions for Biblical Study

In seeking to understand the "religion" of the Bible, it would be well to understand, if that can be done, what religion is. There are various definitions of the word, religion, but the one which perhaps comes closest to the understanding of that term in the biblical tradition and which fits most closely the basic ideas which will be developed in this study is as follows:

> An awareness or conviction of the existence of a supreme being, arousing reverence, love, gratitude, the will to obey and serve, and the like. (*Webster's Collegiate Dictionary,* fifth edition, 1938, p. 840.)

Religion, therefore, is a universal human experience which usually looks outside the human sphere for an understanding of one's life. This understanding is directed toward some power or being with which one can enter a relationship, which will give meaning and purpose and direction to one's existence. This relationship is, generally speaking, directed toward what humanity normally calls "God," and this relationship integrates and subordinates all other facets of experience under its influence. That kind of understanding then leads to a commitment of one's being in the service of the "god" if religion is present. Something like this is to be found in the religious understanding of the biblical writers.

Religion thus understood inevitably becomes part and parcel of the culture and tradition of a people. Therefore to understand the religion of any group, something must be known about the background, history, culture, language, customs, thought-patterns and the like of the group whose religion is being examined. This is certainly true of the "religion" that is contained in the biblical writings. Therefore it is appropriate at the very beginning to set down a few presuppositions for the study of the biblical texts. These following points are especially significant for the study of the Old Testament. Some of these ideas will be modified, however, as the religious thinking of the biblical writers progresses.

First of all, it is a "given" of the biblical writers that God exists. The primitive world did not doubt the existence of powers beyond this world and beyond human endeavor. The Hebrew people, being a part of this primitive world, assumed the existence of a god or gods. There were various ideas connected with the gods of the ancient world. In settled cultures the god usually was identified with a people and/or a country. The nomadic tribes had gods that moved with them, but often it was believed when a nomadic people came into a settled land that the god of that country had priority and authority while these people were in that land. In some cases the god was actually thought to be part of the very *soil* of the country in a quasi-physical sense! (Cf. 2 Kings 5–6)

The gods also had different functions: one was a war god, another a fertility god, etc. And it was sometimes believed that, since circumstances do change, the god who had led a people in the past may not necessarily be the god who should lead the group now. All these different gods with different functions naturally meant that each god had a name. This was true of the Hebrew people as well who called their God (as best as we can determine), Yahweh. The religion, then, of the Old Testament could well be classified (as some do) under the title Yahwism.

It was also believed that the gods could and did exercise control over events in the historical sphere. This belief could vary from the idea that a god controlled *all* events to the idea that only in certain "crisis" situations did or would the god intervene. But it was an accepted premise that the gods could and did control to some degree the events of human history.

Therefore, the existence of a god or gods was not the issue with primitive society or in the religious development of the Old Testament. It was rather the struggle with the question of what was this god like and what did he require of the people. This is in essence what the Old Testament is about, namely, the "revelation" (making known) of Yahweh. What is he like? What does he require? Is he a god of consistency? If so, what kind? How is he different from the other gods? This understanding, as the reader can see, took a long period of time to develop, especially since the Hebrew people took the revelation from the events of their own history (primarily) to hammer out the portrait of Yahweh which finally emerged after almost a thousand years.

Another closely related aspect to keep in mind is that to the people of the ancient world, this universe was *not* a closed system. While there were laws which governed the universe and which could be relied upon for consistency in the affairs of human history, nevertheless there was no thought of a closed system of cause and effect which could not be altered or even abrogated from without by forces that were beyond the knowledge of human intelligence or understanding. What the ancient people could not understand by their own knowledge or standards, they interpreted as "miracles." These miracles were not considered extremely unusual in their time. For those people it was not unusual or unexplainable happenings as such that were important. What was more important was the meaning of these events. What significance did they have? The interpretation placed on the miracles brought them into the religious sphere. For example, in the biblical accounts God can and does intervene in the affairs of human history, never capriciously but always in accordance with his character and always in some relationship and with some purpose toward his people.

A third presupposition for biblical study is strange to many of us in this epoch of human history. We have emphasized so much the value and worth of the individual and the individual's rights that we have neglected the importance of the group. The ancient world did not have this kind of emphasis on individualism. Rather, the *group* was the most important aspect of life, and the group and its interests were always to be placed before the interests of any individual. Laws were written to protect individuals, but for the broader benefit of the group, and individuals were important but important within the context of the group. The survival of the group, clan, tribe, nation, etc., was the most important item.

This emphasis is evidenced quite often in the Old Testament texts and has been called by one scholar (followed by many others), H. Wheeler Robinson, the idea of "corporate Personality."[1] The basic thrust of his argument is that the individual and the group in the Old Testament are so closely intertwined that the group *was* the individual and the individual *was* the group! We do not think this way, and the concept is somewhat difficult for us to understand. It is probably best illustrated by the story of Aachen in Joshua 7. Here we see the group punished because of Aachen's sin—the entire group sinned! And we see the punishment on Aachen meted out not only to him but to his entire family—a sentence that seems overly harsh to us but in the context of the time was viewed as just.

Thus we need to bear in mind that while the individual was important in the Old Testament writings, it was the group or nation that counted the most. And it was only the individual who helped the group or hurt the group who was in essence singled out for close survey.

Further, any religion that is worthy of the name has some concepts or ideas about the "after-life." This was true of the Old Testament writers as well. It is difficult for many to imagine, but the Old Testament writers believed only in a concept known as "Sheol." It was thought that deep in the inner recesses of the earth was a "place of the dead" where the "lives" of persons went when they died. There were no distinctions or differentiations there between rich or poor, good or bad, king or pauper—all came here when physical death occurred. Sheol was a place of gloom, darkness, and dust, and while life was not snuffed out (the Old Testament did not believe in annihilation) existence there was the weakest, palest kind of life one could imagine. One can readily see why some called the "people" there "shades" or "shadows."

There were no rewards or punishments either! Because of this belief the Old Testament writers developed the idea that rewards and/or punishments would be meted out *in this life*. This led to a "theory" that if one did what Yahweh wanted, the person or group was rewarded; but if not, the person or group was punished. This particular kind of thinking permeates *most* of the Old Testament books in one way or another. If one were successful, it was a sign that Yahweh had blessed the person (or group); if one suffered misfortune, it was a sign that something was wrong in that person's life—in fact a "secret" sin may even have been committed!

The essential point here is that rewards and punishments had to take place while the person was living, because in Sheol all had the same kind of fate. This led to the belief (closely related to point three above about the "group") that it was extremely important for the dead to have a "link" to the land of the living. Therefore the *levirate* law was established which made it a *requirement* for the next of kin (a brother preferably) to "visit" the widow for the purpose of raising up a child for the deceased if he had died childless. They believed that, in this way, a connection between the deceased and the land of the living was established so as to in some way lessen the dreariness of Sheol. This did not necessarily mean that the widow married the next of kin, and it was not a license for sexual promiscuity. Once the conception had occurred, the relationship was over unless marriage then took place. Even so, that child was considered to be the child of the deceased.

Another concept that deserves some mention at this point is the primitive idea of "Holy War," the idea that wars were waged in the name of the god for his benefit or at his command. Anything that was captured in such a war was to be *totally* dedicated, i.e., sacrificed, to the god. This included spoils, cattle, and people. This dedication of the spoils of war to the god was known as *ḥerem* (or *cherem*), also called being under the "ban." This may surprise some who have always felt that "Thou shalt not kill" was an injunction for pacifism, against capital punishment, and the like. But the commandment meant simply, you shall not commit unlawful murder! There were capital crimes in Israel designated by law, and killing in war was quite acceptable.

Magic has always played a part in the history and religions of primitive peoples, and this was no less true in the culture out of which the Old Testament arose. There are numerous places in the Old

Testament where magical motifs still exist, and the most frequent type is that of "sympathetic" or "mimetic" magic. This kind of motif is found when humans (usually priests or other religious persons) perform an act which seeks to insure the accomplishment of a purpose. This act is not to their way of thinking a *symbol* (as we would interpret it) but an actual part of the accomplishment of the goal. For example, if one wants rain, what better way to insure the result than by performing a ritual act that includes pouring out of water? (As we shall see later, the so-called "prophetic signs" fall into this category.)

Another example may be taken from the fertility religions which were quite prominent in the ancient world. In settled societies that were dependent for existence on the crop and the fertility of the ground, it was only natural that people should be preoccupied with ways to make the land fertile. Myths arose to explain the cycles of nature; many of these had a god who was killed but rose after being dead for a while. When he came back to life, he usually had sexual relations with his consort which insured fertility in the earth. Under the impetus of sympathetic magic, the fertility cults developed temples with cult prostitutes to insure the fertility of the land. Young women served in these temples as acts of devotion to the god and to the community. There was even a name for them, *kedashah,* to distinguish them from the ordinary street prostitute, *zonah.* The word *kedashah* is a derivative of the Hebrew word for "holy" which basically means "set apart, other." Therefore the cult prostitute was "set apart" for the god.

The spoken word had special significance also in primitive thought. It was believed that the words had within themselves a certain power which could accomplish the intent or meaning of the spoken statement. This is the reason why one had to be very careful in blessing and cursing because, once said, the words could not be recalled.

This same idea lies behind the reluctance of the people to pronounce the personal name of their god. Since the Hebrew language is written by means of consonants (vowel signs were added much later), Yahweh's name was YHWH. And lest the name be said incorrectly or used (even inadvertantly) in an unacceptable way, the Old Testament people used the pronunciation of the word for Lord, Master *(Adonai)* for the "tetragrammaton" as it came to be known.[2] By the New Testament period even this was too close for comfort, and many ways had been devised to keep from referring directly to Yahweh. For example, the Rabbis would refer to God as "The Holy One, Blessed be He"; also, the term "Heaven" would be used metonymously to refer to God. The use of the third plural indefinite was also utilized to stay as far as possible away from any misuse of the words for God or Yahweh. Looking ahead, one can already see how shocking it was when Jesus came along referring to God as *Abba,* the Aramaic equivalent of "Daddy"!

It was a part of the ancient world of the Orient that the practice of "hospitality" was viewed as a serious matter. When one sat down to eat with a person, this meant that both the host and the guest pledged themselves to each other for at least as long as the food may remain in them! This usually was taken to be about three to four days. During this period the bond of protection and friendship must remain intact at all costs. A number of Old Testament stories take on some added dimension when the reader bears this in mind (cf. Genesis 19:8; Judges 4,5). The significance of the New Testament communal meals take on a new dimension when viewed in this way as well.

Much has often been made of the idea that the God who is revealed in the pages of the Bible is a God of *love.* The New Testament idea of *agape,* love, is known even to those who know little else about the religion of the Bible. Too often, however, this love has been given a new content by our own culture and thinking, for love has been sentimentalized either into a slushy concept of extreme self-depreciation, or an idealized view that love conquers all! Neither of these two extremes fits the biblical picture.

The term most often used in the Old Testament is *ḥesed.* This Hebrew word has been variously translated as mercy, love, steadfast love, or in some other way, but basically has within it the idea of "loyalty to a covenant." While the idea has a definite concept of affection and concern and personal relation, the meaning is primarily one of responsibility and commitment. It would be wrong to think that the term or the Old Testament idea lacks any emotional attachment. Love in the Old Testament (and in the New) is never simply emotional attachment but always is rooted in responsible commitment in a personal relationship.

And while the New Testament concept of *agape,* self-giving love, is probably a bit more on the emotional side, it is no less true of *agape* than it was for *ḥesed* that the basic idea is that of commitment and responsibility. In other words, there is no such thing in the Bible as love that is "free," with no strings attached. The biblical view of love always has responsibilities attached that are exceedingly weighty, for the God of the Old and New Testaments demands total commitment and responsibility from those to whom he has offered himself in special relationship. This love, this new relationship, cannot be earned; it is certainly not deserved; and it must be accepted on the terms of the Giver! There are in almost every religion obvious attempts to "manipulate" the deity, but in biblical thought this cannot be done.

Finally, it should be emphasized again that the Old Testament writers believed that Yahweh was active in the affairs of this world order, in history, if you will. They did not think that everything that happened was a result of Yahweh's direct action, but they did believe that human events, especially the significant ones, could be interpreted in the light of Yahweh's activity in the human process. But this activity was never the result of whim; it was rather Yahweh active in history in accord with his own being. This is why the Old Testament is so much the unraveling of *what kind* of God Yahweh is rather than philosophical discussions about whether he exists. As one American biblical scholar has appropriately written: "The belief that God is to be met first of all in the world of history is Israel's most remarkable contribution to theology. . . . The alternatives to revelation in history are revelation in nature and in thought. . . . The permanent contribution of Israel lies in her emphasis upon the priority of the historical approach, for it was the God who was known in history who was later to be found in other spheres, and not *vice versa*. . . . If we are to believe in God at all, this is really the only kind who is worth believing in. The God of philosophy serves a useful function in helping to fill up the blank spaces in human thought; belief in the God of nature gives us, like Wordsworth, a satisfying sense of the numinous when we contemplate nature's wonders; but only a God whom men first met in the disasters and triumphs of human history is able to speak to men in the depths of their being when they too are involved in the clash of historical forces. This is the God of ancient Israel."[3]

Canon and Literature

The biblical writings have been composed, edited, and compiled over a long period of time. At first, naturally, the stories about Yahweh and his dealing with the Hebrew people were transmitted orally. How long this process went on we do not know; but after some time people began to record the relationship of Yahweh with his people in written form. Other documents were written as well. In fact, some of these were utilized by the biblical writers in the composition or compilation of their work and are specifically mentioned in the texts (cf. Joshua 10:13; 1 Kings 11:41; 1 Kings 14:19; 1 Kings 14:29), and others can be detected by close scrutiny of the documents. Several of these will be studied in the course of this book.

Further, as with any literary collection, there are various kinds of literature included in the Bible. There is historical narrative, poetry, saga, drama, religious fiction, and other types as well. It is always important when interpreting any work to know what kind of literature one is dealing with. For example, one must not treat poetry in the same manner as historical narrative. At the appropriate places, most of these types will be discussed as the various books are examined.

It is important, however, at this point to discuss Hebrew poetry since so many Old Testament writings are poetic or contain poetic passages. The essence of Hebrew poetry is not basically rhyme or rhythm, even though these are present, but its basic characteristic is "parallelism," a rhyme or rhythm of thought. The Hebrew verse is composed of two lines. The first line makes a statement and the second line "relates" to that statement. The way the second line "relates" determines the nomenclature for the parallelism.

(1) The second line restates the meaning of the first line. This is called *synonymous* parallelism.

O LORD, rebuke me not in thy anger,
nor chasten me in thy wrath. (Psalm 6:1)

(2) The second line states an antithesis of the meaning of the first line. This is called *antithetical* parallelism.

O Let the evil of the wicked come to an end,
but establish thou the righteous . . . (Psalm 7:9a)

(3) The second line builds upon the meaning of the first line. This is called *synthetic* parallelism.

> For the wicked boasts of the desires of his heart,
>
> and the man greedy for gain curses and renounces the LORD.
> (Psalm 10:3)

It is imperative that the reader understand this type of writing, for as in almost any language the poet must be allowed "license" to express meaning and ideas.[4]

It is important for the reader who is attempting to understand the religious teachings of the biblical books to keep in mind that in spite of all the critical, analytical questions which detailed work on the texts involves, it is best to examine each book or collection of books as a whole. In this way one does not miss the important points, themes, and motifs of the final writer(s) or editor(s). This method of interpretation is exceedingly important for at times the scholar engrossed in detail "misses the forest for the trees"!

One further area needs to be mentioned. Just when did these books come together in the form in which we now have them and when were they accepted as "authoritative"? No one knows precisely the answer to every aspect of the process of the formation of the *canon* of the Old and New Testaments, but it is generally accepted that the first five books of the Old Testament were compiled into their approximate present form by about 400 B. C. These books were considered authoritative by the Jewish community and were called *Torah* (*Instruction,* sometimes erroneously thought to be simply *Law*). By about 200 B. C. the prophetic books had been collected and compiled and were accepted as authoritative in addition to the Torah. They were divided into two groups, the Former Prophets: Joshua, Judges, Samuel, and Kings; and the Latter Prophets: Isaiah, Jeremiah, Ezekiel, and the Book of the Twelve. The designation for these books is *Nebi'im* (the Hebrew word for prophets).

Following the period 200 B. C. and into the Christian era there was a great deal of writing done, so much so that there was a bewildering variety of religious ideas and motifs. After the fall of Jerusalem to the Romans in 70 A. D. and the destruction of the Temple there, and in the face of the growing Christian movement, there was held at Jamnia in 90 A. D. a council of the Rabbis which recognized those other books considered authoritative for the Jewish faith to be accepted along with the Torah and Prophets. This group was called the Writings *(Kethubim)* and contained the remainder of the books we now know to comprise the Old Testament canon.

While the Old Testament canon was closed after Jamnia, the large number of other writings did not disappear. And it is a great blessing that they did not. Many were preserved in various stages and languages, so that there is a large body of literature known as the *Apocrypha* and *Pseudepigrapha* of the Old Testament. *Apocrypha* is a technical name given to that collection of books which did not get into the Old Testament canon but are found in Greek translations of the Old Testament. The term *Pseudepigrapha* formerly referred to all other "Intertestamental" writings, many of which were written under pseudonyms, thus the name Pseudepigrapha. After the discovery of the Dead Sea Scrolls, another group of writings was added to this list. All of these plus the Rabbinic literature (which we shall discuss later) give a rich insight into the history and religious thinking of the period from 200 B. C. to 100 A. D.

It is probably already evident that in the English Bible the order of books in the Old Testament is different from that which we have outlined. This situation came about when in the third and second centuries B. C. it became necessary for the Jewish people to have a Greek translation of their Scriptures. By this time many Jews were scattered throughout the Roman Empire and did not speak nor understand Hebrew. Therefore, in order for these people to have access to their authoritative writings, it was necessary to begin to translate these documents into a language the people did understand. This Greek version of the Old Testament is called the *Septuagint* (sometimes designated LXX) because traditionally the work was purported to have been accomplished by seventy persons. By the time that the process was completed, not only had the translators translated the Hebrew into Greek, but they also had attempted to arrange the books in what they felt was chronological order. This scheme was followed by Jerome, translator of the Latin Vulgate, and later by the English translators, thus giving the order popularly known today.

The period of history covered by the New Testament writings is not really as long, since all of the New Testament books were written within a one hundred year span ca. 50–150 A. D. Each book at first had a separate history, but gradually collections began to be made first of Paul's letters, then the grouping together of the four Gospels, and later other epistles and writings. As with the Old Testament, there were many more writings than these. In the face of growing heresies, various attempts were made to select those writings which the early Church accepted as authoritative. In 367, Athanasias, a church leader at Alexandria, published a letter setting out the twenty-seven books which he felt were authoritative. By the end of the fourth century it was generally accepted that these were authoritative for the Christian Church. Those other books which did not find a place in the New Testament canon are called the New Testament Apocrypha and are valuable for helping to ascertain what other kinds of literary works and religious thinking were known and used during the early development of the Christian Church.

Additional Readings

Bible: Selected chapters from Psalms and Proverbs

Secondary Material:

Harshbarger, Luther H., and John A. Mourant. *Judaism and Christianity: Perspectives and Traditions.* Boston: Allyn & Bacon, Inc., 1968. Cf. especially pp. 1–31, 62–130.

Wright, G. E., and R. H. Fuller. *The Book of the Acts of God.* Garden City, New York: Anchor Books, Doubleday & Co., 1960, pp. 1–43.

Ryken, Leland. *The Literature of the Bible.* Grand Rapids, Michigan: Zondervan Publishing House, 1974, pp. 13–30.

Filson, F. V. *A New Testament History: The Story of the Emerging Church.* Philadelphia: The Westminster Press, 1964, pp. 390–94.

Souter, A. *The Text and Canon of the New Testament.* Rev. by C. S. C. Williams. London: Gerald Duckworth & Co., Ltd., 1954, pp. 137–87.

Notes Chapter 1

1. H.W. Robinson, *Corporate Personality in Ancient Israel* (Philadelphia: Fortress Press, 1964), Facet Books, Biblical Series, #11. This short pamphlet includes Professor Robinson's original article which first appeared in 1935 as well as another later article which clarifies the concept further.

2. The horrible mutation, Jehovah, is a result of the German transliteration of YHWH combined with the vowels of the word *Adonai,* yielding Jehovah. In its day this probably was an innovation which aided persons in learning that God in the Old Testament had a personal name. But it should not be used today.

3. R.C. Dentan, *The Knowledge of God in Ancient Israel* (New York: The Seabury Press, 1968), pp. 230–33.

4. It would be beneficial for the reader to examine the Psalms, Proverbs, and other books for exercise in acquainting himself with Hebrew poetry. In some Bibles this is difficult since the poetry is *not* printed in poetic form. The RSV has done this, however.

2
Religion to the Conquest

One of the most difficult problems in dealing with the development of the religion of the Bible is encountered immediately. This is the problem of attempting to ascertain exactly what kind of religious beliefs were accepted in the Patriarchal period, i.e., up to the Mosaic covenant. When one examines the nature of the sources, it is not too difficult to understand why confusion exists.

It is clear from a detailed study of the first four books of the Old Testament (the Tetrateuch) that there were three basic sources used in the final editing and compilation of these books. Scholars generally designate these sources as J, E, and P. Incorporated within each of these sources were probably other sources, both oral and written, thus adding to the confusion. The mixture of all these elements makes it especially difficult to isolate any consistent pattern in the early stories about the old Patriarchs as to their specific religious ideas.

At this point it is helpful to examine briefly these sources. The oldest of these is J, dating from the tenth to the ninth century. The author of this epic work is called the Yahwist because he uses Yahweh as the name of God throughout. Writing in Judah perhaps in the time of Solomon ca. 950 B. C., this author presents a "history" of God's dealing with the Israelite people from the creation of the world to the entrance into Canaan (perhaps even further). He seems to have been the first to connect the Mosaic traditions with the older stories of the Patriarchs, a major interpretative insight. The style of the writing has numerous peculiarities, enabling the reader to determine and trace the pieces of the work through the Tetrateuch.[1] Because of its early date

there are many points at which Yahweh is depicted in an-
thropomorphic and anthropopathic terms (i.e., attributing the form
and feelings of human beings to God), and there are many points
where the writer seems to be possessed of a primitive naïvety which
is indeed refreshing. Yet in all this the Yahwist understands that
Yahweh is the Lord of creation and history. Yahweh is a Personality,
a living Person who enters into relationship with his creation. The
Yahwist is also very realistic especially when dealing with the great
heroes of the faith, for he makes no attempt to cover or conceal their
sins and weaknesses (cf. Gen. 12:10–20; 27; 34; Numbers 21:10–13).

Another prominent feature of the J account is the emphasis
(which is seen clearly in these early books) on aetiology. Every society,
especially more primitive ones, has a natural curiosity about why
certain things are as they are. The stories which attempt to give such
explanations are called aetiological. Such questions as why does the
snake crawl on its stomach, why is there pain in child-bearing, why
does man work so hard to scratch a bare and meager existence from
the earth, and others are addressed in some of these ancient and
primitive stories. It must also be remembered that these stories were
not meant to explain the questions scientifically but rather religiously.
Such aetiological accounts are found in the other sources also, but
most are located in the J writer's epic.

The second source is designated E because the basic term used for
God is *Elohim.* (In fact the Elohist holds that the Hebrew people did
not even know the name, Yahweh, until the time of Moses.) This work
probably originated in Northern Israel after the division of the kingdom in 922 B. C. It was the northern parallel to the work of the
Yahwist. After the fall of the Northern Kingdom this work was
probably taken to Judah where someone(s) combined J and E into one
work,[2] and much of E was preserved as one can determine by the
number of "doublets" which are found in the biblical texts.

This writer however, is characterized by a high moral tone which
is seen in his tendency to "whitewash" the sins of the heroes and by
the fact that it is he who preserves the Decalogue. And it is he who
further emphasizes the covenant-motif as the chief ingredient in the
religion of Israel.

It is puzzling to some that J depicts Israel worshiping Yahweh

from the very beginning while E introduces the name at the time of
Moses' call. This may well be explained by the fact that the Northern
tribes and the Southern tribes were in origin different peoples, the
Northern people being Aramaean and the Southern being Amorite
(two "families" of Semitic stock). Abraham is identified with the
Southern areas, while Jacob is identified with the Northern areas. It
was the Northern group which went into Egypt, participated in the
Exodus, and later (after the "conquest" of the land) was joined with
the Southern group. The Yahwist would then be reflecting the traditions of the South, and the Elohist the traditions of the North. And
it is interesting that the editors did not feel it necessary to conceal any
differences or to harmonize the accounts!

The last major source is called P because it is concerned with
"Priestly" ideas, the cultus, and proper modes of worship. This source
was probably compiled during or immediately after the exile (ca.
550–450 B. C.). Its emphasis is basically on the cultic and ritual
practices of the nation. There is less narrative than is included in
either J or E, and the emphasis is on the covenants, especially those
with Noah, Abraham, and Moses. The work itself is held together
basically by genealogy. Much of this source is valuable only for the
study of the customs and rituals of the Hebrew people, but the Priestly
writer(s) excels at one point. He believes in the absolute sovereignty
of God as above all creation. This is clearly seen in the P account of
creation (Gen. 1:1–2:4a) which opens the biblical text and sets the
stage for the remainder of the story of God's dealing with humankind.

The Early Beginnings

The editors or redactors of the Torah attempt to present an account
of the history of the dealing of God with the people by tracing this
history all the way back to the very beginning. The P account of
creation is a magnificent picture of God towering over all, making
order out of chaos, and finally creating human beings, male and
female, to rule over all the created order.

The J account of creation (2:4b–3:24), while not as majestic as the
P story, nevertheless holds to the same theology even though the
account is much more primitive and naïve in many respects. The
naming of the animals represents the same motif as in P, that man is

to have control over the created order. All that has been created is for the purpose of witnessing to God's majesty and serving human needs.

But part of J's account is given over to what is wrong in the world. The serpent (not the Devil) asks the woman about the trees. When she replies that they may eat of any tree except the tree of knowledge of good and evil (probably meaning knowledge of everything), the serpent tests the woman at humanity's most vulnerable point—the highest created being or subordinate always wants to "take over." "You will become as God." The rationalizing process begins and finally ends in expulsion from the garden. Even here according to some there is mercy in Yahweh's judgment—"lest they eat of the tree of life and live forever." The greatest punishment is to be struck immortal in sin![3]

From this point to the end of the Primeval history (Gen. 1–11) the editors depict humanity as growing deeper and deeper in its sin. The increasing sinfulness of humanity which is really not stopped, only delayed, by the judgment of the Flood, means that another way of dealing with the human race must be established. This comes with the selection of Abraham, the leader of a small clan, to be the means whereby ultimately God's purpose for his created order may be accomplished.

God's purpose is for all people to "know" him, i.e., to experience him in an intimate, personal way. To achieve this goal God "elects" persons to carry out this purpose. Gen. 12:2–3 (paraphrase): "And I will make of you a great nation, and I will bless you, and make your name great, so that you will be a blessing . . . and by you all the families of the earth will be blessed." This is the reason, the rationale, for the selection of Abraham. And it is this theme that is constantly reiterated throughout the pages of the biblical writings. Election, as it is sometimes called, is a very important doctrine of the biblical writers, even more important than the ideas connected with salvation! Abraham is chosen by Yahweh for a purpose—to make Yahweh known throughout all the earth. He had been "elected" or "chosen" to carry out that duty, and a covenant was established between Yahweh and Abraham to seal the agreement.

Historically speaking the Patriarchal narratives (Gen. 12–50) are much debated among biblical scholars. Are these stories about real individuals, or individualized stories about tribal movements, or are they simply legendary imaginings of an ancient people about their more ancient past? It is not our task here to dwell on these problems, but it may be of interest to the reader that since the archeological findings at Mari and Nuzi (ancient cities in Assyria and Babylonia whose cultures flourished about the same time as the Patriarchs) we do know that many of the *specific* customs and rituals depicted in the Genesis accounts were indeed practiced in the ancient world of that precise historical period.

It is similarly difficult to determine precisely the nature of the religion of the Patriarchs. The most widely held view at this time is the thesis of A. Alt,[4] who argues that the patriarchs were founders of different cults in which each of them was given a name linked with the name of the deity (cf. Gen. 15:1; 31:42, 53; 49:24). That these persons did practice a type of clan religion is probably undeniable but *exactly* what kind of religion they held is still something of a mystery. According to the stories, however, there are certain definite religious motifs that stand out in spite of any uncertainty otherwise. The religion of these leaders was characterized by faith, i.e., trust in the deity, by an understanding of the deity as a Person with whom one could enter into a relationship, by an understanding that the deity required certain codes of conduct, and that he was genuinely concerned for the well being of the human race. At least that much seems to be clear.

One further aspect is apparent also from the reading of Genesis. The concept of covenant which reaches its apex in the Moses account in Exodus is also made a theme motif in Genesis. The covenant made with Noah is a prelude for the covenants Yahweh makes with each of the Patriarchs. Covenant was a part of the culture of that time. Persons entered into agreement and pledged themselves to a particular set of obligations for which they would receive certain services and/or favors in return. These covenants could be made between equals or non-equals (a king and a vassal, for instance). The covenants between God and man are of the latter type, but the important point religiously is that this Yahweh was willing to enter into agreements with human beings, and to be bound by certain conditions provided that the human element kept its part of the bargain.

The promises to Abraham, to give him the land, to make of him a nation, and to cause him to prosper, are all writ large in the narratives dealing with him and his successors. At the end of Genesis Yahweh has saved his chosen group from the famine of the time, but they are in Egypt, not in the land promised to them.

The Exodus

Every movement has a focus, and the religion of Israel is no different. The exodus from Egypt, viewed as Yahweh's mighty act of deliverance on behalf of his people, is the focus for Hebrew religion. All points forward to it; all looks back toward it. From the beginning of the history of Abraham in Genesis 12 the movement has been toward this great climactic act of God. The words of Exodus set the stage, "There arose a Pharaoh who knew not Joseph." The oppression of the people is portrayed in a few short but graphic verses. The delightful hand of the old-time storyteller is obvious to the reader. Yahweh causes the very person who will ultimately "defeat" the Egyptians to be reared in the very house of Pharaoh.[5] The hero, Moses, suffers from his own stupidity and rashness, and leaves the land of Egypt. In a faraway place, having married and settled down, he suddenly sees a marvel, a bush burning but not consumed.[6] In this experience Moses is called by Yahweh to lead the people out of Egypt as another stage in the fulfilling of his promise to Abraham. Moses is less than overwhelmed by this invitation and asks what this god's name might be.

In the ancient world names had a special significance. The name was supposed to reflect something about the actual character of the person, and to know someone's name gave a special power over the person whose name was known. And it was thought that for one to know the god's name would give that person a kind of power over the god as well!

The name that is then given to Moses has been translated in many ways: "I will be what I will be," "I am that I am," and others. Some scholars have attempted to derive the meaning through etymological studies and have come up with "Blower," "One Who Fells," "Storm God," and on and on.

It is the opinion of this writer that the meaning is to be found partly in linguistics and partly in how the name and its meaning developed in the history of the Hebrew faith. The root word is היה, which basically in Hebrew means to be, to become, to happen. It is not usually used in terms of static being but in terms of dynamic growth. The Hebrew verb form indicates a causative type of action. Thus the translation could well be something like, "I will cause to happen what I will cause to happen." This meaning seems to fit better the Old Testament understanding of Yahweh ("He who causes to happen"), and at the same time takes any control over him away from human beings. If, indeed, he is the one who in and of himself causes to happen, even knowing his name will not grant power over him. This is one of the distinctive ideas of the Old Testament concept of Yahweh. Whereas in most religions of the ancient world, the devotees attempt to gain control over the deity, in the Hebrew faith Yahweh never allows this. It is always on Yahweh's terms that he enters into agreement with the people; and it is he who has control over history and the created order; it is always he who knows what is best for his people; and it is his will that is to be accomplished in this world order.

The promise made to Moses is that Yahweh will be with him, not that the task will be easy. And the purpose for the deliverance from Egypt and the call of Moses is the same as that of the call of Abraham, that Yahweh's name (i.e., himself) may be made known in the world.

The story of Moses' encounter with the Pharaoh of Egypt and the subsequent plagues is well known. It is interesting to note in passing that no one source lists all ten plagues: J has seven, E has five, P has five. It is also interesting, however, that each source (as best we can determine) contained the first (water into blood) and the last (the death of the firstborn). After the plagues the people were allowed to go. Just how many left and which way they went are technical questions which need not concern us here. However, it is likely that it was a small motley group that departed. They were a stubborn and "stiff-necked" people who sorely tried the patience of Moses. They crossed the "Sea of Reeds" (the Red Sea is a later interpretation), and the Egyptian chariots, according to J, mired down in the swampy ground. It was the P account which idealized this episode into the walls of water on the right hand and on the left hand (Ex. 14:29).

The important point to remember is not so much *exactly* what happened but what the happening meant to these people. To them revelation, the "uncovering" of the Personality of their God, came through the combination of the event plus the interpretation of that event. One can say historically that at some point in time a small group of Hebrews escaped from Egypt, wandered in the wilderness, and finally entered into the land of Canaan. Revelation does not enter the picture until someone interprets this as the hand of God, leading this people, showing to them what kind of God he is, and what the purpose was in these occurrences.

The Exodus events were the formative ones for the establishment of Israel's religion, and the elements here are basic for the development of the faith. It would appear that at least three points are clear: (1) It is Yahweh who is the Lord of the historical process; (2) He is a God who wishes to enter into a covenant with the people; (3) There is a purpose in his activity.

In order to understand better these and other elements of the Mosaic religious tradition, one probably is best served by examining the Decalogue. There are several aspects which should be kept in mind. This code is set in the style of "apodictic" or "absolute" law in contrast to most Old Testament laws which are conditional in nature (If . . . then . . .; cf. Ex. 21–23, Leviticus, etc.). Further, there is the introduction to the Decalogue which sets a magnificent framework for these requirements. "I am [Yahweh] your God, who brought you out of the land of Egypt, out of the house of bondage" (20:2). These commands are secondary to the One who gives them. In other words the Law is rooted in an act of redemption, a gracious, loving act on behalf of the people.

There is a popular misconception that the Old Testament is a book of law and rules while the New Testament is a book of grace and love. Both Testaments, however, claim to be a revelation of the same God who, while righteous, just, and holy, is nevertheless a God of mercy and feeling. This God is one who cares about his people and his created order and about the world and where it is going. And this is no less true in the Old Testament writings than the New.

20:3—"You shall have no other gods before me." Great debate has been exercised in the past as to whether Moses or the Mosaic covenant was "monotheist." In the technical sense, i.e., the absolute denial of the existence of other gods, the answer is probably No. There is no absolute assertion as to the sole existence of Yahweh as God until the exilic period, but the Hebrew covenant excluded the worship of any god but Yahweh. Some insight may be gained by comparing this with the most likely translation of the great dogma of the Hebrew faith, the Shema (Deut. 6:4), "Hear, O Israel: Yahweh is our God, Yahweh alone." But implicit in this injunction were the seeds which, if cultivated, would lead inevitably to the absolute conviction that Yahweh was indeed God alone.

20:4—"You shall not make for yourself a graven image. . . ." It is a unique feature of this faith that it resisted the trends prevalent in the ancient world to make images. This commandment is probably a derivative and intensification of the first to ensure the worship of Yahweh alone. A secondary aspect of this command is the threat/promise contained in it. If we remember the idea of "corporate identity" (cf. pp. 15–16), this becomes somewhat easier to understand. Also if one is realistic about such matters, it is true that the good and bad of the parents and community *are* passed on to the children and through them to their children. Even here there is the concept of Yahweh as a merciful God because the evil is visited only to the third or fourth generation, while the covenant-loyalty and mercy are shown to thousands.

20:7—"You shall not lift up the name of [Yahweh] to *nothingness.*" The last word in the command is difficult to translate accurately from the Hebrew into English. It means basically trivia, vanity, nothingness. The injunction here is a warning against the use of the *name* (which has power within for good *or* ill) in anything other than the most appropriate way. This fear led to the people not pronouncing the name at all! (Cf. p. 18.)

20:8—"Remember the seventh day, to keep it holy." The origins of the Sabbath are lost in the dim misty recesses of the past, but the tradition probably goes back to the Babylonian area and is connected with good and/or evil days. It is, of course, baptized into the Hebrew faith by becoming a day holy to Yahweh. (One notes that the P creation account is structured around the Sabbath motif!)

20:12—"Honor your father and your mother." This is really self-explanatory. Remember the corporate personality motif, however, and the importance also of retaining a link with the land of the living.

20:13—"You shall not kill." This command forbids unlawful killing but is not to be used as a "proof-text" for pacifism or against capital punishment. Both war and capital punishment were accepted in Israel.

20:14—"You shall not commit adultery." Adultery in ancient Israel could only be committed against a husband. If a wife had relations with another man, the husband was the wronged party. If a husband, however, had relations with a married woman, adultery was involved but only against the woman's husband—not against his wife! This injunction attempted to keep the family secure and probably also had some background in the idea of the offspring being a link between the parent and the land of the living.

20:15—"You shall not steal." The sanctity of a person's property was recognized as a basic tenant of the Mosaic faith.

20:16—"You shall not bear false witness against your neighbor." Perjuring in a trial is strictly forbidden. It is interesting to note that two witnesses were required to agree in their testimony in a law court (cf. Deut. 19:15f.). After all, what good is rule by law if anyone can bring any charge on the flimsiest of evidence? Or if the law courts were corrupt (cf. Ex. 23:1–9)? Violation of this command eroded the very foundation of their society.

20:17—"You shall not covet your neighbor's house." *Anything* that belongs to one's neighbor is not to be coveted, for covetousness is the ground for all kinds of malicious actions (cf. Paul in Romans 7), and practically speaking endangered the unity of the group.

Thus the "Ten Words" as they are sometimes called touched upon man's relationship with both Yahweh and the neighbor. As we have tried to indicate, these are not cold rigid commandments but rather bold, broad principles by which one should direct one's very life! Neither are these simply *external* rules to be obeyed in outward form only, but rather, as has been stated, internal principles by which one can order and structure the relationships which are most meaningful in human existence.

The majority of the remainder of the Tetrateuch is given over to laws and ritual observations. Most persons are familiar with the story of the golden bull (Ex. 32), the wanderings in the wilderness and the accompanying discontent and even rebellions of the people (Num.

10–36), and the fact that Moses himself was not allowed to enter the promised land (cf. Num. 20:2–13).

At the conclusion of Numbers, Israel is almost ready to launch her attack on the land of Canaan. The covenant has been established, the basic rules and principles accepted, and a new leader, Joshua, has assumed command.

Additional Readings

Bible: Genesis 1–50; Exodus 1–20; Deuteronomy 1–6, 29–34.

Secondary Material:

Anderson, B. W. *The Beginning of History: Genesis.* Bible Guides Series. Nashville: Abingdon Press, 1963.

Hunt, Ignatius. *The World of the Patriarchs.* Englewood Cliffs, New Jersey: Prentice-Hall, Inc., 1967.

Vawter, Bruce. *A Path Through Genesis.* New York: Sheed and Ward, 1956.

Notes Chapter 2

1. For a detailed listing of J, cf. N.K. Gottwald, *A Light to the Nations* (New York: Harper & Row, 1959), pp. 215–18.

2. The specific process by which the sources were combined into the Torah is a complicated one. For further study cf. H.H. Rowley, ed., *The Old Testament and Modern Study* (Oxford: The Clarendon Press, 1951; paper edition 1961); C.R. North, "Pentateuchal Criticism," pp. 48–83.

3. Cf. G. von Rad, *Genesis,* trans. J.H. Marks, Old Testament Library Series (Philadelphia: The Westminster Press, 1961), p. 94.

4. Cf. Albrecht Alt, *Essays on Old Testament History and Religion,* trans. R.A. Wilson (Garden City, N.Y.: Anchor Books, Doubleday & Co., Inc., 1969). "The God of the Fathers," pp. 1–100.

5. The word "Moses," even though it is given a Hebrew etymology, is really an Egyptian word. It means basically "son" and is incorporated into many familiar Egyptian names known to us—Thutmose (son of Thut), Ahmose, Raameses, and the like.

6. It is common in the Old Testament writings for fire to be used as a symbol of the Presence of the deity. This is called technically a "theophany," an appearance of God. This usually occurs when God is present in a particular place at a particular time for a particular purpose. Cf. Gen. 15:17; Ex. 13:21–22; 1 Kings 18; etc.

3
The Religion of the Conquest and the Kingdom

The basic source for our information about the "official" religion of this period of Hebrew history (ca. 1100–586 B. C.) comes from that block of material known as the "Deuteronomic History." This compilation of writings and tradition began with the book of Deuteronomy which is cast as a sermon (really a series of sermons) of Moses to the people before they enter the Promised Land and concludes with the exile of Judah. The entire work contained what we know as Deuteronomy, Joshua, Judges, Samuel, and Kings.

The basic theological motif which holds the work together is that if the nation is faithful to Yahweh, it prospers; if not, it is punished. The cycle of *apostasy, judgment, repentance,* and *deliverance* is the hallmark of the Deuteronomic history, and this structure is most obvious in the books of Judges, 2 Samuel, 1 and 2 Kings. When the nation was loyal to Yahweh, it prospered; when idolatry entered the picture, the nation was judged.

The book of Deuteronomy was composed or compiled from sources which were probably circulating in the Northern Kingdom before the fall in 722/1. The work has close affinities in theology and style with the source E. When the Northern Kingdom fell, many of its literary sources probably made their way to Judah and to Jerusalem. A portion of this work was found in the Jerusalem Temple in 622 B. C. when Josiah was king. As far as scholars can ascertain, probably at least chapters 12–26 and 28 of our present book of Deuteronomy were involved since the ideas contained in these writings became the foundation for the Deuteronomic Reform (about which we shall say more later).

The books of Joshua and Judges give differing accounts of the "conquest" of the land. Joshua depicts it as swift and decisive, while Judges shows a more gradual taking over of the territories. There is probably some historical truth in each of the views, but our interest is primarily in the type of religious organization which we find.

It is argued by a large number of scholars that the Hebrew tribes after entrance into the area were organized as an "amphictyony." In this arrangement tribes are loosely bound together with a common bond based on their "religion." When one tribe needed aid or was attacked militarily, the others were supposed to respond with assistance. There was to be a central sanctuary which served as the focus for the organization. With the Israelites, at first this center was at Shechem, but later it was located at Shiloh.

It was at Shechem that Joshua renewed the covenant with the people. This event is preserved for us in Joshua 24, where Joshua recited the history of Yahweh's dealings with the people and charged them sternly to choose which of the gods they would serve. They chose Yahweh and the covenant was renewed. One of the interesting aspects of this episode is that there was extended to others the opportunity to worship Yahweh even though they had not taken part in the Exodus and had not worshiped Yahweh before.

The book of Judges is such a delightful book in many ways that it is unfortunate that many of the stories cannot be discussed in detail. As has been mentioned, the stories in Judges reflect less than an ideal situation for the people of Israel. Those were times of anarchy and trouble, perhaps best illustrated by the recurring statement, "In those days there was no king in Israel; every man did what was right in his own eyes" (21:25). That is a dangerous and scary situation at any time! Religiously speaking, however, the stories in Judges show the superiority of Yahweh over the gods of the land as well as in the usual Deuteronomic theology.

Mention should be made here of the part that sacrifices and festivals played in the religion of Israel. While it is undoubtedly true that sacrifice was practiced in the Patriarchal period and in the wilderness wanderings, it is also probable that the emphasis on sacrifice and the development of the different types took place after the people had settled in the land of Canaan. In fact, many of the festivals and sacrifices can be traced to a Canaanite origin.[1] It is also probable that these were not considered absolutely necessary at first. However, with the passage of time, the people more and more came to view these actions as obligatory, and since obligatory as having power within themselves to accomplish their purpose apart from any real change on the part of the devotee. As we shall see later the prophets (and Psalmists) opposed this view vehemently.

The books of Samuel and Kings are primarily a history of the monarchy and the unification of the Northern tribes and the Southern tribes into one nation under David and Solomon, and then as divided kingdoms until the exile of each. As one would expect, the Deuteronomists judge everything by their usual standard. Apostasy leads to judgment in the Deuteronomists' view, and this was the cause of the split in the kingdom since Solomon had erected altars and shrines for the gods of his various wives! The great sin of the North is idolatry (the bulls set up at Dan and Beth-el), and similar sins and actions are committed in the South as well. Finally the apostasy was so flagrant that the two nations were judged by being taken into exile.

At this point it is well to take note of the history of this period of Israel's development since it will serve as a framework in which to fit the prophetic movement. Next to Moses, these great personalities called prophets have left more of themselves in the religion of the Old Testament than any other group or person.

Rise of the Monarchy

As already noted, the situation in Canaan was at the time of the Judges very tenuous for the people of Israel. The tribes were ill-organized, at best loosely connected, and the land had little or no real political unity so as to give a measure of stability and order to the people. Everyone doing what was right in his own eyes led to anarchy and chaos (cf. Judges 17–21).

Nevertheless there was among the tribes of Israel a strong feeling that to have a king was an act of idolatry. Yahweh was to be their ruler; human kings made great demands on the people and freedom, so recently won, might disappear (cf. 1 Sam. 8:10–18). There were others who felt also that Yahweh should be their ruler but that the existential realities demanded some kind of leader, like a king, who could unify the country and organize defenses against the new invaders in the land, the Philistines, who fought with iron weapons. This struggle is reflected in the passages in 1 Samuel 8–12.

The central figure in this transition period is Samuel, who was a priest, a prophet, and a judge. It is he who anointed Saul as king over Israel even with his own misgivings about that action. Saul, from the tribe of Benjamin, is truly a tragic hero. Obviously looking the part of a great leader, he ultimately proved to be less than the man for the job. He did, however, begin the process of unification of at least the Northern tribes and was successful against the Philistines. He attempted to be an ardent Yahwist, but he ran into trouble with Samuel when he officiated at a sacrifice when Samuel did not arrive on time (1 Sam. 13), and when he did not carry out *in full* the requirements of the ḥerem (1 Sam. 15).

Samuel then anointed David to be king over the people, and while Saul sought to kill the young man, Saul's son, Jonathan, became David's friend. David was the real founder of the United Kingdom, but this process took some time and much intrigue not all complimentary to David.

Saul and Jonathan died fighting the Philistines on Mt. Gilboa while David and his "ragtag" army of outcasts had joined with the Philistines. (They did not participate in this battle, however.) When word came to David of the death of Saul, he immediately mourned and even delivered a moving elegy (2 Sam. 1:19–27). He then moved to Hebron in the south and became king over Judah. Much activity followed in the north in connection with the struggle for power to succeed Saul. David demanded of Abner (Saul's commander of the army) that Michal (Saul's daughter to whom David was married earlier) be returned to him. The fact that she was now married to someone else did not matter. This gave David a claim to the succession in the eyes of the ancient world. Joab, David's commander, then killed Abner; Ishbaal (or Ish-bosheth), Saul's son, was murdered. These events prepared the way for the Northern tribes to come to David to ask him to reign over them (2 Sam. 5). Needless to say, he accepted!

David then captured the old Jebusite fortress of Jerusalem, made it his capital city, and brought the Ark (the symbol of Yahweh's Presence) there as well, thus making this neutral city the new political and religious capital of the United Kingdom. Finally, he inquired if there were any of the house of Saul left. Only one, a crippled son of Jonathan, was found. David brought him into his home. (What better place to keep an eye on the only remaining person who could be the rallying point for a revival of the political ties of Saul with the north!)

With the kingdom united David continued to make secure the nation and its boundaries. He conquered the Philistines, the Moabites, the Edomites, and other surrounding countries. The larger powers (Assyria and Egypt) were busy with internal problems, and thus Israel was riding a crest of political greatness.

It would be unthinkable not to single out one of the major sources for the Deuteronomic historians' work. In chapters 9–20 of 2 Samuel and in chapters 1–2 of 1 Kings, most scholars are agreed that we have one of the oldest pieces of historical reporting of any length in the ancient world. This section is usually called the "Court History of David" or sometimes the "Succession History." Many believe that it was written by an actual eyewitness of the events, and the author gives an intimate picture of the last days of David's reign and the problems and intrigues involved with the succession.

When the intrigues had cleared, Solomon, Bathsheba's son, had emerged as the successor to his father even though he was not the eldest nor a son of one of the more "legitimate" wives. It is interesting to note that the prophet Nathan, who had delivered the word of Yahweh's judgment to David about the Bathsheba affair, now sided with her and was instrumental in helping to make Solomon the ruler.

The nation grew even more and prospered further under Solomon and his public works' projects. The great powers (Egypt and Assyria) were still preoccupied with their own troubles and the United Kingdom enjoyed relative peace and prosperity. Of religious significance, Solomon built the temple to Yahweh and under him the wisdom movement (to be discussed in some detail later) began with court backing. He married the daughters of many foreign rulers to cement political alliances. The fact that he had 700 wives and 300 concubines did not bother the Deuteronomic historians, but the erection of altars and places of worship for their gods did! (Cf. 1 Kings 11.)

When Solomon died, his son Rehoboam succeeded him and came to Shechem to be certified as king by the Northern tribes. Under Solomon the Northern peoples had begun to grow restless. Solomon had devised a system of twelve "districts" (which were not congruous with the old tribal districts) for purposes of taxation, forced labor, conscription, and the like. When the Northern leaders came to Shechem, they asked that changes be made. Rehoboam's older advisers counseled yielding to the demands; his younger advisers counseled a "get-tough" policy. He accepted the latter advice and the Northern tribes, under a leader named Jereboam, seceded from the union! And they made it stick, since Egypt took this time to make a minor advance into Southern Palestine, which occupied Rehoboam long enough for the Northern state to be solidified. From this point to the exile, the Northern state is called Israel, and the Southern, Judah. The split occurred in 922/1 B. C.

Jereboam attempted at once to give the Northern kingdom a political center at the old amphictyonic capital of Shechem and made religious centers at Dan and Beth-el by erecting images of golden bulls at each. This action was anathema to the ardent Yahwists not only because there were to be no images,[2] but also because the symbol for the Baal worship of the land which was still very much present was the bull! The Deuteronomic editors constantly refer to this action as *the* major sin of Israel (cf. 1 Kings 14:7f.; 1 Kings 16:25f.; 2 Kings 10:29; etc.).

The two kingdoms remained approximately equal for the first fifty years of their separate status, until a strong king named Omri (876–869) took over the throne in Israel. Because of its superiority in population, economics, and geographical location, the Northern state naturally became a stronger and more influential entity. Omri moved the capital to Samaria, which he made into a strong fortress. Humanly speaking, Omri was one of the greatest kings of Israel, but the Deuteronomic historians gave him short space!

Ahab, his son, succeeded Omri and continued the political growth which his father had begun. He established close ties with the Phoenicians and cemented that alliance by marrying Jezebel, the daughter of the Phoenician king. Infamous for her evil, she is nevertheless one of the most admirable characters in the history of Israel. A strong, domineering woman, she was a power behind Ahab, who had a tendency to be less than aggressive at times.

During this period the nation of Assyria had begun to establish itself and to move westward. Syria and Israel and others banded together to check this movement and met Shalmaneser III in a great battle at Qarqar in 853. This coalition of small states, while not defeating the Assyrian army, did check its westward movement for the time. Not long after, however, they were fighting among themselves again, and in 850 Ahab was killed fighting against the Syrians.

Discontent, much of it religiously motivated, had been building against the Omrid dynasty, and in 842 a bloody military revolution was accomplished by a general named Jehu. All the Omrids were slaughtered, which meant that political ties with other countries were broken and most of the qualified leaders of the country were eliminated. Israel during this period was little more than a vassal state of Syria, its immediate northern neighbor.

Assyria, however, had begun to move again and in 802 defeated the Syrians, but surprisingly enough left Israel to itself. Israel then under Jehoash (801–786) and Jereboam II (786–746) recovered its lost territory, renewed treaties, and a new wave of prosperity swept over the land. This prosperity led, unfortunately, to a distinct class situation in Israel and a corrupt political and judicial system. When Jereboam II died the country was plunged into periods of anarchy. Coupled with this was the rise of a new king in Assyria, Tiglath-Pileser III (745–727), who began another westward movement. This was not for the purpose of exacting tribute as his predecessors had done, for this time the king was more interested in permanent conquest.

In order to fight this growing menace, Israel and Syria headed an alliance of smaller nations which banded together to attempt to keep the Assyrians out of their lands. Judah refused to join and was invaded by the alliance (the Syro-Ephraimitic alliance) for the purpose of forcing her to join. The king of Judah, Ahaz (against the advice of Isaiah), appealed to Tiglath-Pileser for aid. In 733 Pileser destroyed the coalition and took over control of Northern Palestine and the Transjordan area, but when he died in 727 the vassal king of Israel, Hoshea, withheld tribute and appealed to Egypt for aid against Assyria. In 722/1, Samaria, after holding out for two years, fell to Sargon II of Assyria, who then deported many of the people to other lands and imported peoples from other lands to settle in Israel.

With this the history of the Northern kingdom came to an end. The people who remained intermingled with the foreigners brought in, and these people were always looked upon with disgust by the people of Judah as "impure." Those who were carried to other lands did the same wherever they were taken and blended into the culture of their new homes.[3]

We turn now to the history of Judah. Off the beaten path between Egypt and Assyria (and Babylon), this kingdom survived longer than Israel, even though economically speaking it was never as prosperous nor politically influential.

One of the interesting aspects of its earlier period was that the son of Jehosphaphat was married to the daughter of Ahab and Jezebel, Athaliah, who introduced the worship of Baal into Jerusalem! Her son, Ahaziah, was killed in the Jehu purge of the Omrid house, at which time she seized the throne and tried to have all those of the royal Davidic line killed. The infant son of Ahaziah was saved by the priests of Yahweh and at the propitious moment was proclaimed king. Athaliah and the chief Baal priest were both put to death; she was the only non-Davidic ruler to sit on the throne of Judah (cf. 2 Kings 11).

Uzziah (783–742) was the king in Judah whose time and fortunes paralleled the era of prosperity under Jereboam II in Israel. After him, however, there were hard times and domination by Assyria. Ahaz, who succeeded Uzziah, had appealed to Tiglath-Pileser for help when attacked by the Syro-Ephraimitic alliance. In those days a political alliance meant more than simply political self-interest. It meant that the lesser state had to adopt the religion of the superior state, so this alliance with Assyria was also an act of idolatry. To pay the heavy tribute demanded by Assyria, Ahaz had to increase taxation, and much land was lost. Social decay and moral laxity prevailed. The clergy were corrupt and became "yes-men" for the king. It was during this time that there arose a longing for a king who would be like David. Time had passed and the idealization process had wiped out the bad memories. David was now the great figure of the past, politically speaking, and people were longing for something better.

Hezekiah (715–686) came to the throne; he instituted cultic reforms, in essence an announcement of rebellion against Assyria. Sennacherib (immortalized by Byron) did not take this lightly and moved quickly into the area. He devastated the countryside and, except for a mysterious occurrence, probably would have captured Jerusalem. Isaiah counseled Hezekiah not to fear the Assyrians, and in time Sennacherib left to return to his homeland. The religious interpretation was that the angel of Yahweh had slain the Assyrians. Herodotus, the Greek historian, recounts this episode and states that the rats ate the bowstrings of the Assyrians![4] At any rate, this episode gave impetus to the idea of the doctrine of the inviolability of Jerusalem which practically became a dogma after these events.

The worst king of Judah (and the one who reigned the longest) was Manasseh (687/6–642). Under his kingship pagan worship flourished; social corruption was prevalent and the prophets were driven underground. Even child sacrifice was practiced during his reign! It was a period of hard times for the Yahwists, and it was no small embarrassment to the Deuteronomic writers that Manasseh reigned so long.

In 640 the child, Josiah, came to the throne, and it was during his reign (622) that a "book of the law" was found in the Temple which was being repaired (2 Kings 22). This document was read to Josiah, who was so moved that he used it as the basis for a sweeping reform. He summoned the people to the Temple for a covenant renewal ceremony, and afterwards made provision for many changes. Of course all pagan cults and practices such as astral worship, Baal practices, magic, divination, and child sacrifice were strictly forbidden. But the basic feature of the reform was to centralize all legitimate worship in the Jerusalem Temple. This centralization gave some control over the type of worship which went on. Even the Passover, which had been celebrated in the home (when it *had* been celebrated), was also moved to the Temple. In order not to put priests out of work, rural priests were admitted to participate in the cultic practices at the Jerusalem Temple (cf. Deut. 18:6–8).

Josiah was aided in this move by the decline of the Assyrian state which was now being menaced by the rising power of Babylonia. By 612 Nineveh, the capital of Assyria, had been destroyed, but Egypt, wishing to keep a balance of power, now came to the aid of Assyria.

In 609 Pharaoh Necho (Neco) went to assist Assyria, and Josiah, siding with Babylonia, marched to meet him at Megiddo. For his efforts Josiah was killed; a vassal king (a son of Josiah, nevertheless), Jehoiakim, was placed on the throne by the Egyptians—and Josiah's reform collapsed.

In 605 Nebuchadnezzar of Babylon had defeated the Egyptians at Carchemish and overrun Palestine, and Judah again became a vassal of Babylonia. But Jehoiakim, encouraged by the Egyptians, rebelled once more (600 B. C.). By the time Nebuchadnezzar could get around to this problem, Jehoiakim had died (598) and his son, Jehoiachin, was on the throne. In 598/7 the city surrendered and many of the leaders of the nation were carried into exile to Babylon. Jehoiachin's uncle, whose name was changed to Zedekiah, was placed on the throne by Nebuchadnezzar. Shortly thereafter Zedekiah also rebelled against Babylonia along with other small nations in the area. By 588/7 Jerusalem was under seige and in 587/6 the city was burned and the walls leveled. A second deportation then occurred.

After this a certain Gedeliah was made governor over this area. He was killed by a radical group who then fled to Egypt. It is possible but not certain that a third deportation took place at that time (582), but after these events the land was incorporated into the large province of Samaria.

The Deuteronomic history ends with a look at Jehoiachin in exile, being treated kindly. It was probably their way of saying that there was still hope for the nation since the Davidic line was still alive.

Additional Readings

Bible: Joshua 1–10, 24; Judges 1, 4–5, 6–9, 21; 1 Samuel; 2 Samuel; 1 Kings; 2 Kings

Secondary Material:

Heaton, E. W. *The Hebrew Kingdoms.* The New Clarendon Bible Series, Vol. III. London: Oxford University Press, 1968.

Notes Chapter 3

1. For a masterful discussion of this topic cf. Roland de Vaux, *Ancient Israel: Its Life and Institutions,* trans. John McHugh (New York: McGraw-Hill, 1961).

2. Most scholars are agreed that the bulls were representatives of the *throne* of Yahweh and were not meant to represent Yahweh himself.

3. The theory that these exiles somehow wandered around finally making their home in England has no foundation in fact whatsoever. This is sometimes called the Anglo-Ephraimitic theory.

4. The mention of the rats may indicate that some form of plague spread through the army.

4
The Prophetic Movement

One of the most exciting, interesting, and influential of all religious movements occurred during the period of the "statehood" of Israel. This is, of course, the prophetic movement which belongs to this particular period of history and is almost meaningless apart from it.

The phenomenon of prophecy is not unique with Israel or Yahwism, and its precise backgrounds are lost in the "misty recesses" of the past. There are, however, several theories about how prophecy developed in Israel. Older scholarship detected a three-stage process in the development of prophecy. The first stage was that of the "seer," those persons who attempted to divine the future. The second stage was that of the *nebi'im* (Hebrew for "prophets") composed of roving bands of persons who were characterized by ecstatic seizures. Such a seizure was supposed to be the sign that the god or the spirit of God had descended upon the person. While in this state the person was to receive a message from the god which would be announced either during the time of ecstasy or after the seizure had departed. The third stage was that of the classical prophets who appeared for the most part from the ninth to the fifth centuries B. C. In earlier times these were called the "writing" prophets, but this is a misnomer, since their words were transmitted orally for a period of time until the accounts of their work and words were written down by later disciples.[1]

A second theory holds that there were two basic types of prophet in the ancient world, a "seer" type which was basically connected with nomadic peoples and an ecstatic type basically connected with the fertility cults. In Israel these two types gradually came together, were transformed by the influence of Yahwism, and evolved into the great movement which is depicted in the books of the Old Testament.[2]

As valuable as these schemes are, the great probability is that many tributaries have fed into the main stream which became known as the classical prophetic movement. And because of the inspiration, genius, and courage of these persons the whole is greater than the sum of its parts! There are elements of the old seer, the ecstatic, and the diviner in Hebrew prophecy, but many other elements are involved as well. There is a priestly connection with the prophets, a wisdom connection, and a connection between the court counselors and the prophets. The movement is complex and varied, but essentially the one ingredient which made this movement so great was the prophet himself and his belief that Yahweh had called him to deliver a message to the people.

For a long while in biblical interpretation the prophets were viewed as predictors of the future; then they were viewed as innovators to such a degree that some even argued that Old Testament religion would not have survived without them; they have also been depicted as great social reformers. There is some truth in each of these ideas, but the prophets should be interpreted primarily as religious personages who felt an unyielding loyalty to Yahweh and who believed that they were announcing Yahweh's word to the people. That they did speak about the *immediate* future is true; that they did add a dimension to Old Testament religion that we should be impoverished without is also true; that their message had direct implications for society and social ideas is not to be denied. But primarily *religion* is their "bag," and all these other aspects are only relevant when based upon that foundation. They were intense individuals and they acted in "unusual" ways quite often. Perhaps Bruce Vawter has summarized the situation best when he says,

> There was little room in this placid pastoral scene [speaking about some of the Victorian commentators] for an Elijah slavering in the throes of ecstatic seizure, an Isaiah walking mother naked as a warning to Egypt, an Hosea agonizing over his prostitute wife, an Ezekiel cooking over cattle dung to drive home a point, or even an Amos addressing the respectable dowagers of the parish as fat cows. With the flair of the born journalist, Ernest Renan toward the end

of the last century caricatured the prophets as the first radical pamphleteers. Even serious students of the Bible, particularly those infected by sociology, have not entirely shed the illusion that the prophets were grass-roots economists, distributionists, or political dilettantes of one color or another. We still read of them as spear-heading a movement of return to the "nomadic-peasant" ideal; which is indeed curious, since it would be hard to imagine two classes of men more traditionally opposed in their aspirations than the nomad and the peasant.[3]

What we have here is a group of people, each of whom believed that he had been summoned by Yahweh to speak His word to the people and that this word is not really something new but a re-kindling of the Exodus covenant and traditions. In their commitment to these motifs and their application of them to a new age, they did in fact add much.

Even though Moses is called a prophet (Deut. 34:10f.) the first real contact that we have with prophecy is in 1 Samuel 9:9 where we read, "He who is now called a prophet [*nabi'*] was formerly called a seer [*ro'eh*]." In this setting we find roaming bands called "sons of the prophets" which were characterized by frenzied ecstatic activities.[4] After this we find prophets in the court of the king serving as political as well as religious counselors (Nathan with David, for example), and groups of prophets connected with the royal court (cf. 1 Kings 22). These different persons with differing functions seem simply to be a part of the culture of the time. But with Elijah we find the transitional figure who is usually considered to be the forerunner of the "true" prophet. This weird character from the desert came into the court of Ahab and announced that there would be no more rain (1 Kings 17).

The background for the confrontation between Elijah and Ahab lies in the religious struggle at that time. Jezebel, Ahab's wife, had championed the worship of the Tyrian Baal and had persecuted the prophets of Yahweh. The basic question to Elijah was very simple: which god is to be worshiped in Israel, Yahweh or Baal? And it is interesting to note that in the stories which surround both Elijah and Elisha the superiority of Yahweh over Baal is central. These stories "are not the work of simple people, but by a well informed author who was intimately acquainted with Canaanite mythology and protested against it by showing that all powers in heaven and earth are under control of Israel's God. The miracles discharged by Elijah as increasing the oil and meal, withholding or releasing the forces of rain, restoring the dead to life, ascending heaven, were designed to undermine the belief prevalent in Canaanite circles that Baal was the dispenser of all these blessings."[5]

Even the name of the prophet reflects the emphasis, Elijah = Yahweh is my God! The conflict in the confrontation was resolved after a three-year drought and the encounter at Mt. Carmel (1 Kings 18). The pouring out of the water was probably originally an act of sympathetic magic, and the fire is, of course, the theophany which depicted the Presence of Yahweh. The rain then came and from this point on the question of who is God in Israel was never really encountered again, at least not to the same degree. Yahweh was to be worshiped in Israel, but Baal worship did not die easily and many features of the Baal cult were gradually incorporated into the worship of Yahweh. This was one of the chief "irritations" to the prophets who followed.

The books of the Old Testament known to us by the names of the prophets whose words are supposedly contained therein are many and powerful. These persons were in older times known as the "writing" prophets, but scholarship has long since discovered that this is a misnomer. The prophets themselves did not write; they spoke.[6] And their words were passed down from generation to generation orally until they were collected together, written down, and then finally reached the form in which we now have them. The larger books seem to have a definite pattern: (1) oracles against the nation; (2) oracles against foreign nations; (3) oracles of hope. These elements are also found in the smaller books, but not in the same order, and in addition we find stories about the prophets themselves contained in many books. Most of the prophetic books are written in poetic form since this seems to be the way the prophets spoke.

One problem that should be noted here is that of how the people in those times determined between true and false prophets. It should not be difficult for us to imagine what confusion there must have been in the mind of the average person when two prophets, both claiming to have the direct word from Yahweh, gave exactly opposite oracles![7]

There were certain criteria which needed to be met to determine exactly through whom Yahweh was speaking. The most obvious "test" was that of fulfillment (cf. Deut. 18:15–22). Further, the true prophet appealed to the traditions of the past and based his argument on the *content* of his message set in the historical context of the moment. Is this message in "concert" with what was known of Yahweh? Was this action consistent with what was known about Yahweh's nature and commandments? Is what is being said "realistic"? All these aspects and others as well were part of the scene, but in the final analysis it was only after the haze of history had lifted that the words of these fearless men were seen to be true and right!

Prophets to Israel

There are two prophets whose works have been collected who spoke to Israel before its fall in 722/1. Amos, a "foreigner" from Judah, and Hosea, a native of the land, spoke in the last years of that nation.

Amos came upon the scene ca. 750 B. C. in the time of the great, but hollow, prosperity under Jereboam II. The book bearing his name was arranged so that the attention of the reader is focused immediately on the enemies of Israel (cf. Amos 1:3–2:5). After a series of oracles against the foreign nations, Amos then turned his message towards Israel. Chapters 2:6–6:14 contain basically oracles against Israel, and chapter seven begins a "biographical" section dealing with narratives about Amos and visions which he has had. The book concludes with promises of hope.

Amos is a fine example of pre-exilic prophecy. He saw the evils of his time as they were manifested against the backdrop of Yahweh's commands. Because the nation had turned its back on Yahweh and his covenant, judgment must inevitably come.[8] The people had gone beyond the point of no return.

The book of Amos reflects the prophet (from Tekoa in Judah) as a person totally convinced of his call to speak in the name of Yahweh (3:8b; 7:14–15). His message, as is the message of each prophet, is to a specific situation with implications for the *immediate* future.

Amos' religious emphases are as follows:

(1) Yahweh is more than simply the God of Israel. He has concern for and control over *at least* the nations surrounding Israel (cf. 1: 3–2:3; 9:7).

(2) The nations are judged in accordance with the amount of knowledge (revelation) which they have. The sins enumerated in Amos' announcement of Yahweh's judgment, these *extreme* acts of cruelty (1:3–2:3), are in themselves beyond the moral bounds of what even the pagan nations accepted and acknowledged as "proper." "There are therefore fundamental rules expressing God's will for the relationship between nations; Yahweh punishes transgressions of those rules even when Israel is not involved."[9] Closely connected with this idea is Amos' insistence that the more "revelation" one has, the more God expects. In Amos 3:2 he says,

> You only have I known of all the families of the earth; therefore I will punish you for all your iniquities.

Privilege begets responsibility, and the election by Yahweh does not place Israel in a position of special privilege but rather calls for a total commitment of the people to Yahweh and his covenant.

(3) From the reading of Amos, there must have been current among the people of that time a concept known as the "Day of Yahweh." The people of Israel understood that on that day there would be an action of God which would judge the peoples around them and would establish the nation of Israel as the center of power in the ancient world. But Amos insisted that while there may be a "Day of Yahweh," the nation of Israel could not look forward to such a day because it too stood under the judgment of God (cf. 5:18–20).

(4) There is an insistence in Amos that Yahweh is a God of righteousness. To his mind there were certain standards of right and wrong, good and bad, and Yahweh acted in accordance with his nature which was righteous and good. This is the reason for the judgment and why Israel as well as other nations stood under this "sword of Damocles." Because Yahweh's very nature consists of righteousness, he demands righteousness (right action) from his people.

Amos looked around and saw the injustice in the courts, the persecution of the poor, and the general lack of concern for morals. He proclaimed that Yahweh could not and would not tolerate this kind of behavior from his people. Amos' insistence on righteousness did not come from a humanistic feeling of identity with people nor from a super-guilt complex. It came from his basic understanding of

God. Righteousness, i.e., right action, was to be a characteristic of the people even as it was of Yahweh himself. This righteousness had to be a part of the warp and woof of their very selves; it could not be a superficial facade.

Many find Amos (and the other prophets) to be an opponent of the priests and the religious "machinery." This is probably an overstatement since Amos did not oppose the priests or the worship forms of Israel. What he did oppose was the substitution of these things for the real righteousness which comes from within, not from without. And in attempting to make this point clear, he proclaimed the famous statement that has been identified so often with him:

> I hate, I despise your feasts,
> and I take no delight in your solemn assemblies.
> Even though you offer me your burnt offerings and cereal offerings,
> I will not accept them,
> and the peace offerings of your fatted beasts
> I will not look upon.
> Take away from me the noise of your songs;
> to the melody of your harps I will not listen.
> But let justice roll down like waters,
> and righteousness like an ever-flowing stream. (5:21-24)

(5) There is no hope for the nation in Amos. Many commentators find that he has some slight hope (cf. 3:12; 4:15b; 5:3), but on closer examination these figures are not figures for a restored nation but only fragments to show that once there had been a nation there.

The "happy ending" of 9:8c-15 is much debated among scholars. Some argue that 8c-10 is also a part of Amos' message. A few argue that all these verses should be attributed to him. But as one examines closely this passage (especially vv. 11-15) it is seen clearly that these verses are more appropriate for Judah than for Israel and that the emphasis on the exceeding fertility of the land is an emphasis of the post-exilic period. It is Amos who is correct, not those who find false hope in simply having the commandments of Yahweh as a possession. It is Amos who sees clearly that such a corrupt society cannot and should not continue to exist. When a nation has been built in accordance with a certain standard, and it has fallen so far out of line from that standard, judgment is sure: "And [Yahweh] said to me, 'Amos, what do you see?' And I said, 'A plumb line.' Then [Yahweh] said,

'Behold, I am setting a plumb line
in the midst of my people Israel;
I will never again pass by them . . .' " (Amos 7:7–9).

The prophecy of Amos has been examined in some detail because many of his basic points are to be found in the other pre-exilic prophets. Each prophet had his own particular and peculiar emphases, but each basically followed Amos in proclaiming the judgment of Yahweh on a wicked and sinful nation. (Nothing will really substitute for the reading of each prophetic book, and the reader is urged to read each book at one sitting.)

The second prophet to Israel is a later contemporary of Amos: Hosea, who prophesied over a longer period ending sometime before the final fall of the nation. Hosea is perhaps best known for his marriage to a harlot. Whether she was a harlot when he married her or became one later, or whether she was a cult prostitute and he married her after her period of service, or whether there were two women involved or one, need not detain us here. His marriage is the basic source for his understanding of Yahweh's relationship with his people, and this tragic event was interpreted as a prophetic sign.

Many commentators have attempted to make Hosea the great prophet of love, but this emphasis is greatly exaggerated. Hosea did *feel* the pathos of the situation between Israel and Yahweh much more deeply than did Amos, but he no less than Amos saw that the time was near for the judgment of Yahweh to fall. Whereas Amos emphasized the righteousness of Yahweh, Hosea emphasized the more personal, deeper feelings of relationship. His key words are "knowledge" and *ḥesed*. Knowledge in the Old Testament normally means experience; "to know" someone is to experience them in a close intimate relationship. In such a relationship commitments are made and obligations assumed. Such a relationship involved *ḥesed*, loyalty to a covenant in which personal feelings *are* involved. From his own tragic experience Hosea learned something about the agony of Yahweh who is the husband of Israel, but who has been wronged, unjustly and without provocation. Such a break in a relationship like this has serious consequences.

Hosea does seem to take a step beyond Amos when he emphasized that the wrath of Yahweh was part of his mercy, and that the purpose of wrath was redemption. He did not make the mistaken assumption that many of his interpreters have made, namely that the wrath will ultimately redeem the nation and everyone else automatically. But what he does make clear is that the wrath and justice of Yahweh comes directly from the peoples' rejection of his *hesed*.[10]

Even more than Amos, Hosea attacked idolatry (cf. Hosea 4: 12, 17; 8:4; 13:2; 14:8) and foreign alliances (7:11). And like Amos he deplored the moral condition of the people (4:1-2) and the corruption of the religious leaders (4:4, 8-9; 5:1). He denounced the shallow dependence on the external forms of religion without the underlying substance that transforms human existence:

> ... I desire [*hesed*] and not sacrifice,
> the knowledge of God, rather than burnt offerings. (6:6)

It is obvious from reading Hosea's oracles, however, that he had deep feelings for his land. Even though the nation was "a dove, silly and without sense" (7:11), "a cake not turned" (7:8b), a nation which sows the wind and "shall reap the whirlwind" (8:7), Hosea hoped that it may again someday be reunited with Yahweh (cf. 11:1-9). This was not an assurance in the mind of Hosea, however, but only a faint hope (cf. 13:12-16). What Hosea knew for sure was that judgment was coming and that soon! His own personal grief and experience made him long for something beyond judgment, for relationships restored, for commitments re-affirmed. Perhaps the great scholar Otto Eissfeldt has summed it up best: Hosea ". . . is nevertheless not embittered by such an experience; by it his eyes are opened to the enormity of human faithlessness and sinfulness which certainly makes serious punishment necessary, but can finally only be overcome by the revealing of an even greater love."[11] Hosea probably was not aware of what exactly could happen, but he knew it would have to come from Yahweh, not from humankind!

Shortly after Hosea's prophecy Israel did fall to the Assyrians, and the pointed words of Amos were fulfilled:

> Fallen, no more to rise, is the virgin Israel; forsaken on her land, with none to raise her up. (Amos 5:2)

Prophets to Judah

In spite of the fall of Israel and the lesson that should have taught, in spite of being the recipient of the religious traditions from Israel (i.e., E, the prophecy of Hosea, and probably parts of what came to be Deuteronomy), Judah did not pay heed to the events of history, even though there were prophets in Judah who spoke to the nation as Amos and Hosea had spoken to Israel.

The eighth century prophets in Judah, however, did not face the same kind of problem that encountered Amos and Hosea. The nation here had time to "turn around." It was not too late—*yet.*

The two eighth century prophets of Judah whose works were preserved are Micah and Isaiah of Jerusalem. Micah lived in the rural area which was most vulnerable to being overrun by the Assyrians. He predicted doom upon Israel[12] and upon Judah. To him evil was centered in the cities and therefore God's greatest judgment would fall on the cities.

> What is the transgression of Jacob?
> Is it not Samaria?
> And what is the sin of the house of Judah?
> Is it not Jerusalem?
> Therefore I will make Samaria a heap in the open country. . . .
> (1:5b–6a)

> Zion shall be plowed as a field;
> Jerusalem shall become a heap of ruins,
> and the mountain of the house
> [i.e., the temple] a wooded height. (3:12)

Micah was especially harsh on the religious leaders who led the people astray and yielded to the whims of the people simply to retain their positions (cf. 3:5–8, 11), and also toward the political leaders and others who acted similarly (cf. 3:1–3, 9–10; 6:9f.; 7:1–6).

One of the most famous and well-known quotations from the prophets is attributed to Micah:

> He has showed you, O man, what is good;
> and what does [Yahweh] require of you
> but to do justice, and to love [ḥesed],
> and to walk humbly with your God? (6:8)

In his longing for new leaders who would be "right" for the people, Micah mentioned a king who would come from Bethlehem (5:2f.). This king would be like David and would lead the people as a shepherd. It may well be that this is the first "Messianic" passage preserved in the prophetic books, but Isaiah, a contemporary of Micah, also picked up this strand of thought and carried the idea further. (The idea of Messiah and Messianism will be discussed more fully later; cf. p. 68.)

Even though the first portion of Isaiah's ministry (ca. 746–701) roughly paralleled Micah, his message was somewhat different.[13] There was the same pronouncement of judgment on the sins of the people, and the same threat of military defeat, but Isaiah because of his circumstances saw things somewhat differently. He did not find the situation hopeless. But hope lay only in the people returning to Yahweh and his commands, renewing the covenant, and keeping "faith."

Faith to Isaiah was basically "trust," trust in Yahweh and his promises. Faith was the basis of the relationship between Yahweh and his people; it involved a commitment. "Faith is both a moral relationship and the resolve to commit oneself unreservedly and firmly to that relationship, because of confidence in the trustworthiness of the object of faith. Moreover, it is in a real sense the only source of that inner security which gives to men the strength and steadiness needful amid 'the changes and chances' of this mortal life."[14]

Isaiah believed that the people could trust Yahweh because of his nature: he was the "Holy One of Israel." And this "holiness" meant more to Isaiah than simply that God was "other" than human. It meant that his very nature was just and right and good; but because of that he expected the same kind of conduct and being from his people (cf. 1:2–17; 3:16–4:1; 5; 9:18–10:11).

In addition to the emphases of Isaiah on faith and the holiness of Yahweh, there are two other motifs which figure in his work and which evolved into more prominent "doctrines" as the history of the nation developed. These were the idea of the inviolability of Jerusalem and the emphasis on a "Messiah."

The first of these was rooted in the historical events connected with the invasion of Judah by the Assyrians under their king, Sennacherib. In 701 B. C. this army captured forty-six cities in the country-side of Judah (cf. Micah?) and turned then to beseige Jerusalem. Typically, Isaiah told King Hezekiah that if they would trust Yahweh, they would be delivered. And they were! Whatever the cause (political problem at home, plague in the camp, etc.), the Assyrians returned home (cf. Isaiah 36–37). The deliverance was naturally interpreted as a great act by Yahweh, but unfortunately Isaiah's proclamation in that particular circumstance was viewed by the people as a dogma that Jerusalem could *not* be destroyed, that Yahweh would not allow anything to happen to his own city and dwelling place.

The best known perhaps of Isaiah's proclamations concerns those ideas connected with the concept of a Messiah. "Messiah" in Hebrew means "anointed," and the idea of Messiah derives from the practice of anointing persons to perform special tasks in the service of Yahweh. Priests and kings were anointed primarily; therefore the idea of a Messiah originally arose in all probability from a longing for a new kind of king after the order of an "idealized" David (cf. Micah 5:2f.; Isaiah 9:2f.; and 11:1f.). The specific historical background for this was probably set during the time of Ahaz who had no trust in Yahweh at all (cf. Isaiah 7:1–17), and who had "sold" the nation to Assyria because of that lack of faith. This longing for a good king continued into the post-exilic period, and it is this longing which evolved into what is known as Messianism. These ideas and motifs will be discussed later in more detail.

Perhaps the best way to describe Isaiah's challenge to the people and to understand that he did not feel that it was too late for change is found in his confrontation with Ahaz at the time of the Syro-Ephraimitic war: "Take heed, be quiet, do not fear, and do not let your heart be faint because of these two smoldering stumps of fire-brands, . . . [But] If you will not believe, surely you shall not be established" (7:4a, 9b).

After Isaiah and the better king, Hezekiah, had departed, Judah labored under the reign of Manasseh, who in all probability persecuted the prophets of Yahweh. During the time of his rule (the longest in Judah, a great embarrassment to the Deuteronomic historians!), we hear no prophetic voice, and it was only after his death and during the reign of Josiah that a book of the Law was found in the temple and the Deuteronomic Reform instituted. And it was only then that the voice of the prophet was heard again in the land.

The prophets during this period were Nahum, Zephaniah, Habakkuk, and Jeremiah. Nahum's prophecy was simply an elegy of joy over the fall of Nineveh (612 B. C.), for to him this fall was the proof that Yahweh's justice was executed in history.

Zephaniah is usually considered to have prophesied before the Deuteronomic Reform; in fact, some view him as a forerunner of the Reform. The idea is that this challenge by the prophet led the leaders to act responsibly. Whether either of these is true may be debated, but it is true that the prophetic voice was back and that it was essentially the same as before. Zephaniah reaffirmed the Day of Yahweh concept as Amos had understood it (1:7, 10–16) and castigated those who did nothing and thought that Yahweh will do nothing also (1:12).[15]

Habakkuk probably came along about the time that the threat to Judah was no longer from the Assyrians but from the Babylonians (Chaldeans). The basic struggle of this prophet was: Why would Yahweh allow a nation more evil than Judah to execute his judgment on Judah? Habakkuk really began the questioning of the meaning of life, the Deuteronomic ideas which were quite prevalent in his time, and God's justice. In short, just why is the world this way, and why does God allow things to be as they are? These questions by Habakkuk are in a sense not in line with the prophetic movement but are more a forerunner to the wisdom movement which flowered in the post-exilic period and attempted to struggle with the questions Habakkuk raised.

True to his prophetic heritage, however, he found hope in the nature of Yahweh who has a purpose (cf. 2:14), who is in control of the progress of history (1:14; 2:20), and who calls upon humanity to keep the covenant faith even if understanding cannot be found (2:4).

Upon turning to the prophet Jeremiah, one finds the most human of all the great figures in the prophetic movement, if not the entire Bible! Jeremiah, who prophesied (626–586) to Judah at the time of her fall to Babylon, was a figure of some significance. The book that bears his name was composed of two basic sources, a collection of oracles (1–25) and the memoirs of Baruch, his scribe, about Jeremiah's life (26–45).

Jeremiah has some affinity with Hosea in that he felt very deeply and very strongly about his land and its people. He was at first very hopeful about the Deuteronomic Reform, but soon became disillusioned when he saw that its effects were only superficial. People coupled the aspects of the reform (centralization of worship in the Jerusalem Temple) with their (mistaken) doctrine of the inviolability of Jerusalem and assumed that all was well. Jeremiah made it clear that Yahweh was greater than Jerusalem and the Temple and could do just fine without either. (Cf. chs. 7 and 26.)

To this man, sin was rooted in the perverted hearts (natures) of humankind. He learned that this perversity was not limited to the poor and uneducated but was just as prevalent with the rich and learned and powerful (5:1–5). Passion and lust and greed were the accepted attitudes of the time: "They were well-fed lusty stallions, each neighing for his neighbor's wife" (5:8).

Jeremiah saw that nothing short of a radical transformation could make any changes. His constant plea is for the people to "circumcise their hearts" (4:4; 9:26). But their guilt was so great that even lye would not erase its stain (2:22), and they have done these things for so long that they do not even know how to blush (6:13–15)! Jeremiah was torn between compassion for his people (cf. 8:18–9:1) and utter disgust at their attitudes and behavior (cf. 9:2–3).

Plots were made against Jeremiah (cf. 11:19), and later he was left in a cistern to die (cf. 37–38), because it was Jeremiah's conviction that the exile at the hands of the Babylonians was the true judgment of Yahweh on the people for their sins. But in the exile was exactly where he found hope for the future. Those who had gone to Babylon would be the hope for a restoration and rebuilding of the nation (cf. 24–25). This kind of thinking did not win him any friends among the people. It was looked upon as treasonous!

Even though he predicted doom for the nation there was an element of hope in Jeremiah's thinking. Because Yahweh is the kind of God he is, there was hope in a new covenant. Scholars debate whether the passage 31:31–34 is from Jeremiah or later, but the passage, religiously speaking, is quite compatible with Jeremiah's other ideas and emphases. This new covenant had some very interesting features in that it combined the essential features of the old covenant (the idea of a positive *relationship* with Yahweh and the *purpose* of making Yahweh known to all people) with some new emphases, namely the idea of the forgiveness of sins and the emphasis on the internal transformation of the person.

Jeremiah was finally carried off to Egypt forcibly by some of his countrymen, where according to tradition he was martyred by those he had attempted to help.

With Ezekiel we find another transitional figure in the development of prophecy. Carried off to exile in the first deportation (598/7), this peculiar individual received his call to become a prophet in a vision of Yahweh's throne suspended and transported by a great chariot (chapters 1–2). This occurred in Babylon about 593 B. C. Part of Ezekiel's ministry was conducted before the final deportation (587/6) and part afterwards. It is not surprising, therefore, to find in the book that bears his name elements of the prophets who preceded him and also elements of reflection on the fall of the nation as well as hope for the future.

In spite of the unusual prophetic signs which Ezekiel performed (cf. 3:1f.; 4:1f.; 5:1f.; 12:1f.) and his weird visions, Ezekiel had a profound insight into the greatness of Yahweh. This God was not destroyed when the nation was destroyed; this God was not confined to the land of Palestine but was with the exiles in Babylon. This God was transcendent above the created order; and this God would restore the people to their former relationship with him in the course of time.

There are three basic points of major interest which can be lifted out of the book for emphasis. One is found in chapter 18 where Ezekiel attempted to answer the complaint of the people that they were suffering for the sins of their parents which they did not find just. Ezekiel answered by his famous saying, "The soul that sins shall die. The son shall not suffer for the iniquity of the father, nor the father suffer for the iniquity of the son; the righteousness of the righteous shall be upon himself, and the wickedness of the wicked shall be upon himself" (18:20). On the basis of this passage older commentators often viewed Ezekiel as the great champion of individualism among the Old Testament writers, but upon closer examination it was seen that while Ezekiel did emphasize the individual to a degree not seen before, he nonetheless still found corporate solidarity *the* hope for the people. It was the nation, not individuals, who would be raised (ch. 37); and it was the nation that would be restored (chs. 40–48). Ezekiel seemed to be saying that while individual concerns are right and legitimate, the real question remained one of how the individual was faring in the context of the corporate group. He was at pains to emphasize, as Jeremiah did, that hope for the future lay with the people in Babylon, and he firmly believed that Yahweh would protect and bless his people in exile in this foreign land.

A second major point of interest is that Ezekiel emphasized, as Jeremiah did, the importance of a changed nature. He argued (18:31 and 36:26f.) that Yahweh would make available to the people the opportunity for their receiving a new heart. He would forgive the sins of the people (36:22–25) in order that they could begin anew His elective purpose for them.

Finally, Ezekiel looked forward to a new ruler after the order of David who would shepherd the people in a land where peace and abundance would be the characteristics of the time (ch. 34). But this full restoration could take place only when the people were returned to their homeland, and would center in a new Temple and a new order of worship described in great detail in chapters 40–48. This was the beginning of the emphasis which later culminated in a priestly rule in the post-exilic period.

After Ezekiel and towards the end of the exile in Babylon there arose another prophet who many commentators feel is the greatest of all. We refer, of course, to the Isaiah of the exile, called Deutero-Isaiah, whose work is contained in chapters 40–55 of the book of Isaiah. This prophet predicted the destruction of Babylon and for the exiles an imminent return to their homeland. The historical circumstances had changed; the booming proclamations of the judgment of Yahweh on his people were naturally gone. What mattered now was the care of Yahweh for his chastened people. This prophet predicted a new Exodus (cf. 40:3–5; 41:17–20; 55:12–13) and a restoration in the land promised to their fathers.

As did Ezekiel, Isaiah held an exalted concept of Yahweh as Lord and Creator (cf. 40:12f.), and it was Isaiah who first made the explicit claim (implicit in some of the other prophets) that Yahweh is the *only* God. Here we find monotheism pure and simple.

> Thus says [Yahweh], the King of Israel
>   and his Redeemer, [Yahweh] of hosts:
> "I am the first, and I am the last;
>   besides me there is no god. . . .
> Is there a God besides me?
>   There is no Rock; I know not any." (44:6–8)

Isaiah also believed that the restoration of the nation had a purpose. That purpose was the same as the call to Abraham, that the name of Yahweh may be known in all the earth. The nation was, therefore, called again to its original purpose. Closely related to this motif is the figure mentioned in these chapters known as the "Servant of Yahweh." While the term is used throughout the collection, scholars have isolated four "Servant Songs" as special and perhaps from a different source. These are found in 42:1–4; 49:1–6; 50:4–9; and 52:13–53:12. Perhaps more scholarly ink has been spilled over these verses than any others in the Old Testament.[16] Are these verses from the hand of the original prophet? Who is the Servant—an individual, a group, or both? And under each of these groups, what is the exact identity of the Servant?

We shall not tarry long over these questions, but shall simply point out that the figure of the Servant is not limited to these four passages only and the specific identification of the editor is that the Servant is Israel! (Cf. 41:8f.; 44:1f.; 44:21; 45:4; 49:3.) And in addition many of the characteristics attributed to the Servant are the same as those attributed to Israel.

It is very clear from the text that the task of the Servant is the same as that of the nation:

> I am [Yahweh], I have called you in righteousness,
>   I have taken you by the hand and kept you;
> I have given you as a covenant to the people,
>   a light to the nations,
>   to open the eyes that are blind,
> to bring out the prisoners from the dungeon,
>   from the prison those who sit in darkness. (Isaiah 42:6–7)

> It is too light a thing that you should be my servant
>   to raise up the tribes of Jacob
>   and to restore the preserved of Israel;

> I will give you as a light to the nations,
> that my salvation may reach to the end of the earth. (49:6)

In the pre-exilic period judgment was proclaimed on the nation because the people had sinned, but the questions that had begun to be raised in the exile (cf. Ezekiel) were beginning to occupy more of the thinking of the people and therefore the religious leaders. This question involved suffering *beyond* that executed (and demanded) for sins committed. There could be (contra the old Deuteronomic idea) suffering which was not deserved. What about that?

According to this prophet suffering can be vicarious, i.e., it can be the source and means by which others are healed, kept safe, or escape a greater hardship. This is the theme of the most famous of the Servant Songs, 52:13–53:12. Here was a portrait of an innocent person who suffered unjustly on behalf of others.

> . . . With his stripes we are healed. (53:5c)

> . . . he was . . . stricken for the transgression of my people. (53:8)

> . . . yet he bore the sin of many,
> and made intercession for the transgressors. (53:12c)[17]

Here was a new ingredient in the idea of human suffering in the development of Old Testament ideas. It was not a popular doctrine, but it was one of the answers that had begun to be given to the questioning of people concerning the older idea central to the Deuteronomic theory, namely, that suffering was almost solely for sins committed.

After Babylonia had been captured by Cyrus of Media (one of the most enlightened of all the monarchs of antiquity—and incidentally called by Isaiah, Yahweh's *Messiah* (45:1), the Jewish people were told they could return home. By this time, however, many were settled and prosperous and did not wish to return. But in 538 B. C. a small group under Sheshbazzar did return. The conditions they found upon their return disillusioned them greatly, and the prophets Haggai and Zechariah urged the people to take heart, rebuild the Temple, and all would be well. After some struggle the Temple was rebuilt and rededicated ca. 515 B. C.

Additional Readings

Bible: Amos; Hosea; Isaiah 1–11; Jeremiah 1–7, 31, 36; Ezekiel 1–3, 18, 34–37; Isaiah 40–55

Secondary Material:

Napier, B. D. *Prophets in Perspective.* New York: Abingdon Press, 1963.

Scott, R. B. Y. *The Relevance of the Prophets.* Revised ed. New York: The Macmillan Co., 1968.

Heschel, A. J. *The Prophets.* New York: Harper & Row, 1962.

Whitley, C. F. *The Prophetic Achievement.* Leiden: E. J. Brill, 1963.

Kuhl, Curt. *The Prophets of Israel.* Trans. by R. J. Ehrlich and J. P. Smith. Richmond, Va.: John Knox Press, 1960.

Buber, Martin. *The Prophetic Faith.* Trans. by C. Witton-Davies. New York: The Macmillan Co., 1949.

Hyatt, J. P. *Prophetic Religion.* New York: Abingdon Press, 1947.

von Rad, G. *The Message of the Prophets.* Trans. by D. M. G. Stalker. London: SCM Press, 1968.

Notes Chapter 4

1. Cf. H.A. Guy, *New Testament Prophecy: Its Origin and Significance* (London: Epworth Press, 1947), pp. 1–27.

2. Cf. A. Weiser, *The Old Testament: Its Formation and Development,* trans. Dorothea M. Barton (New York: Association Press, 1961). For a similar approach but with somewhat different details cf. G. Fohrer, *History of Israelite Religion,* trans. D.E. Green (Nashville: Abingdon Press, 1972), pp. 223–29.

3. Bruce Vawter, *The Conscience of Israel: Pre-Exilic Prophets and Prophecy* (New York: Sheed & Ward, 1961), p. 38.

4. This type of activity must have been infectious since Saul himself was caught up with them (cf. 1 Samuel 10:9–13; 19:23–24).

5. Leah Branner, *The Stories of Elijah and Elisha as Polemics Against Baal Worship* (Leiden: E.J. Brill, 1968), p. 140.

6. Cf. Claus Westermann, *Basic Forms of Prophetic Speech,* trans. H.C. White (Philadelphia: The Westminster Press, 1967); cf. especially pp. 90–209.

7. That it was a problem is reflected in the Old Testament itself when prophets disputed among themselves about the will of Yahweh (cf. Jeremiah 27–28).

8. It was a pre-conviction of older scholarship that the pre-exilic prophets were prophets of doom, while the post-exilic prophets were prophets of hope. Therefore, this reasoning concluded, any hope passage in a pre-exilic prophet must be a later post-exilic addition or insertion into the text. While it is definitely true that the basic message of the pre-exilic prophets was judgment, it does not necessarily follow that there could be no hope in their thinking for the people. It is also true, however, that the reader must be alert to the possibility that a hope passage may indeed be later (as we shall see shortly in studying Amos 9:8c–15). Each text must be studied separately and an evaluation made on each individual case without prejudging the evidence.

9. Fohrer, *History of Israelite Religion,* p. 244.

10. Cf. the powerful and brilliant essay by George Adam Smith, "The Sin Against Love," in *The Expositor's Bible,* 6 Vols., ed. W. Robertson Nicoll (Chicago: W.P. Blessing Co., n.d.), Vol. Four, pp. 528–30.

11. Otto Eissfeldt, *Introduction to the Old Testament,* trans. Peter R. Ackroyd (New York: Harper & Row, 1965), p. 391.

12. This probably indicates that Micah's prophetic ministry began sometime before the final fall of Samaria in 721 B.C.

13. The Book of Isaiah as it stands in the Bible (chapters 1–66) contains a large number of collections of oracles and stories from many periods of Hebrew history. Basically the material which revolves around Isaiah of the eighth century is contained in chapters 1–39, but even among these chapters are found oracles from a later period. The nucleus of "First Isaiah" can be found in 6:1–9:6 and 28–31.

14. R.B.Y. Scott, "The Book of Isaiah: Introduction and Exegesis," in *The Interpreter's Bible,* ed. G.A. Buttrick *et al.* (Nashville: Abingdon Press, 1956), Vol. 5, p. 217.

15. George Adam Smith has a pertinent comment on this passage of Zephaniah: "The great causes of God and Humanity are not defeated by the hot assaults of the Devil, but by the slow crushing, glacier-like mass of thousands and thousands of indifferent nobodies. God's causes are never destroyed by being blown up, but by being sat upon." *Op. cit.,* p. 573.

16. Cf. C.R. North, *The Suffering Servant in Deutero-Isaiah* (New York: Oxford University Press, 1956), 2nd ed.

17. Contrary to what many have thought, this is not a Messianic passage and was not interpreted as such by the Jewish people. It was only later that Christians found in this passage the ideal fulfillment in the life and death of Jesus.

5

Religious Development in the Post-Exilic Period

Our knowledge of the period of Jewish history from the return from Babylon and rebuilding of the Temple to the time of the Maccabees (ca. 538–165 B. C.) is very limited. This involved a long period of time in which the people struggled to maintain their identity, and religion played the most important role in that struggle. Most of what we do know comes from the work of a person (or persons) called the Chronicler. The Deuteronomic historians had written a history from Moses to the end of the kingdoms; the Chronicler has written a history from Adam to his own time in the post-exilic period (1 and 2 Chronicles, Ezra, Nehemiah).

As with the Deuteronomic historians, the Chronicler also had certain emphases to make, the chief being that of depicting the people of Yahweh as a theocratic society. Whereas the Deuteronomists emphasized David's *political* strengths, the Chronicler emphasizes David's contribution to the development of the religion, especially religion as it centered in the Jerusalem Temple. While David did not actually build the Temple, the Chronicler depicted him as making all the plans for the Temple. He also did much for the music and administrative aspects (with the Levites) even while he was still alive. It is obvious to anyone who reads the Chronicler's work that it was his conviction that the people were to be organized and governed by the rules of Yahweh, not rules made by politicians.

There are three basic events which should be noted in this period, each of which contributed to the religious development of the times. The first was the rebuilding of the Temple which was completed ca. 515 B. C. It was during this time that we hear the last of talk about an individual Messiah for a long while. Zerubbabel, a kinsman of Jehoiachin, was exalted by both Haggai (cf. Haggai 2:20–23) and Zechariah (cf. Zech. 3:8; 4:1–10) as God's deliverer for the people. All this took place at a time when there were internal problems in the Persian Empire. When the Persian political situation stabilized, we hear no more of Zerubbabel.

It appears from the Old Testament texts that individual Messianism then gave way to the idea of a "Messianic Age," a time when Yahweh would rule, the land would prosper, and the peoples of the world would come to Jerusalem to learn from the Jews (cf. Zechariah 8:1–8, 20–23). The idea of a Messiah originated from the longing for a king like David in the time of 1 Isaiah and Micah. This idea does not really seem to be so widespread as has often been supposed. Both Jeremiah and Ezekiel mention a "ruler" or "Branch," but only in a very limited way. After Haggai and Zechariah looked to Zerubbabel to be the Messiah and this expectation was thwarted, we hear no more of a "Messiah" *per se* in the remainder of the Old Testament writings. But we do find an increasing emphasis on the new age where Yahweh will rule over his people in a setting similar to that outlined above.

The second major development during this period came in 445/4 and 432 when Nehemiah returned to Jerusalem and led the people in rebuilding the walls to the city. There is some confusion in the Chronicler's account as to the dates of Nehemiah and Ezra, but most scholars are agreed that Nehemiah precedes Ezra and that these two were not contemporaries.[1] The confusion probably came about as a result of the fact that Nehemiah lived under Artaxerxes I and Ezra under Artaxerxes II. Nehemiah found the people scattered and helped in rebuilding the walls and giving some order and organization to the city of Jerusalem. When Ezra came he found that the walls were already built, and people in Jerusalem living with an intensity not found in the time of Nehemiah.

Nehemiah instituted some religious reforms especially aimed at keeping the people "pure" from the inhabitants of the surrounding lands, who were viewed as "tainted" both ethnically and religiously.

It was during his time that the governor of Samaria, Sanballat, offered assistance but was rudely rejected. This marked the beginning of the extreme enmity and bitterness between the Jews and the Samaritans which lasted for many years. Nehemiah even forbade intermarriage with the people of the surrounding lands, especially those from Samaria.

This leads to the third major episode, the career of Ezra. As best as can be determined Ezra came to Jerusalem in 398 B. C. "He was a scribe skilled in the law of Moses which [Yahweh] the God of Israel had given. . . ." (Ezra 7:6) He brought with him a book of the law of Moses which he read to the people (cf. Nehemiah 8:1–8).[2] The people confessed their sins and the covenant was again renewed (Neh. 9:38).

Ezra more emphatically than Nehemiah opposed mixed marriages and even broke up marriages that were already consummated and with children (cf. Ezra 10:2–5)! With this leader the character of Judaism changed from a religion outwardly oriented to an inclusive group struggling to survive. So much of his stamp was left upon the ultimate development of Jewish thought that Ezra is perhaps rightly called "The Father of Judaism."

Not only did he change certain ways of approaching life as a religious community but with the establishment of a *written* law, the religion of Yahwism became a "religion of the book." It is too easy to render negative judgments about such a development in what had been a dynamic, vital, and open religious development (at least at its best), but survival was at stake here. And, rightly or wrongly, these leaders, Nehemiah and Ezra, left their stamp upon the religion of the people for a long time to come. And to their eternal credit, Judaism still exists!

Historically speaking, we know relatively little about the development of the Jewish people during the years to the Maccabean period, ca. 168/7 B. C. But we know from a study of other Old Testament books that much was indeed happening with religious ideas and development. There are some prophetic works which exemplify the prevailing atmosphere of the time (cf. Obadiah, Joel, Isaiah 56–66, Malachi, and Zechariah 9–14).

Even though the prophetic movement was "in decline," nevertheless there were a few prophets in the earlier part of the post-exilic period who challenged the people from their lethargy and sin and looked forward to a new age of prosperity and fertility of the land when Yahweh would rule and all the peoples of the earth would stream to Jerusalem for leadership and to learn the law of Yahweh (cf. Joel 2:28f.; 3:17f.; Zechariah 8:20–23; 14:20f.; Isaiah 56:1–8; 60: 1–3, 15–22; 61:5.; 65:17f.). But the historical circumstances that had served as the fertile ground out of which the prophetic movement had grown had changed. The time for chastisement and challenge to turn from sin had become a time for struggling with other issues such as the problems of suffering, the proper methods of worship, the debate over how best to be the people of Yahweh, and even simple survival. Therefore the stage was set for a period of religious ferment in which various kinds of wrestling with religious ideas took place.

One of these developments centered in the worship and worship practices of the Jewish people. Worship was still centered in the Jerusalem Temple, and it was during this period that the Psalter (the book of Psalms) was compiled and edited. The gamut of human and religious feelings can be felt through the reading of these individual units of varying types. There are hymns of praise, laments, thanksgivings, royal (or kingly) psalms, liturgies, and many other types. These originally existed as independent units, were then collected together into five larger units, and finally were combined into the full collection we now have. While some of the Psalms are pre-exilic and some post-exilic, together these poetic expressions reflect the post-exilic community at worship.

Another important development in the area of worship emerged during this period. In the light of the Deuteronomic Reform *real* worship could be practiced only in the Jerusalem Temple. But there were many persons who lived far enough away from the Temple that they were unable to come and participate in the services there. A need for a place of worship was acute, and sometime during or after the exile the synagogue style and place of worship developed. The worship here centered upon the reading of the Torah and the Prophets and an exposition of the passage read. There was also (naturally) prayer and singing. From the synagogue evolved the group of persons known as scribes who interpreted the sacred writings, transmitted the oral traditions connected with them, translated the Hebrew text into the Aramaic language of the people (Targums), and were probably involved in the synagogue schools. These places became centers for religious and community life, and they sprang up in many places since ten male members could organize and constitute a synagogue.

As previously indicated, a strong element in the post-exilic community advocated "turning in" mainly for the purpose of survival for the Jewish people as a distinct entity. But there were those who obviously protested against this kind of thinking and whose works are also preserved for us. The books of Jonah and Ruth are viewed by some interpreters as "protests against exclusivism." The Book of Ruth was set in the period of the Judges and is a delightful tale indicating that even a foreigner (Ruth) can be a person of quality and loyalty, a person who can worship Yahweh ("Your God shall be my God," 1:16), and a person who will keep the laws of the covenant (i.e., the levirate law; cf. 3:1–4:12). Even more shocking was the conclusion of the book where it was asserted that Ruth, a Moabitess, was the great grandmother of none other than King David (cf. 4:16–22)!

The Book of Jonah can also be interpreted as a protest against exclusivism. This is the only prophetic book which is basically a narrative about the life of a prophet or an episode in his life rather than a collection of his oracles. Jonah was called by Yahweh to go to Nineveh, the most hated and wicked and ruthless of all the cities of antiquity. He was to preach to the city. But Jonah decided to flee as far as he could, to Spain (the end of the then known world). A great storm threatened the ship, but the *pagan* sailors did all in their power to save Jonah. Finally, when it appeared hopeless, to appease Yahweh they reluctantly cast him into the sea where a great fish, specially prepared by Yahweh for the occasion, swallowed Jonah. The fish served as both a punishment and a deliverance, for after three days Jonah was deposited on the dry land. The call to go to Nineveh was renewed, and Jonah went. He proclaimed his message and went out on the hillside to see what would happen. A miracle occurred; the wicked people of Assyria repented and Yahweh forgave them. This led to the real heart of the story when Jonah said: "That is why I made haste to flee to Tarshish; for I knew you are a gracious God and merciful, slow to anger, and abounding in [*hesed*], and repent of evil"

(4:2b, paraphrase). The story dramatically and abruptly ended when Yahweh said to Jonah, who was angry over the death of a plant which shielded his head from the sun, "And should not I pity Nineveh, that great city, in which there are more than a hundred and twenty thousand persons who do not know their right hand from their left, and also much cattle?" (4:11).

Both of these works are delightful, humorous, and pointed. Each concludes rather abruptly with little doubt as to the issue the author is raising. In fact it is possible that both of these came from the same circle in the post-exilic period.

Another work which is not exactly the antithesis of Ruth and Jonah but which nevertheless was written to exalt the Jewish people was the book of Esther. This highly romantic type of story was set in the Persian Empire of the fifth century. It told of a Jewess who became the queen and helped to save her people from a diabolical plan to eliminate the Jews. The tables were finally turned, however, and the Jews were allowed to slaughter their enemies![3]

It can easily be seen from these examples that the thinking of the post-exilic period was divided between the idea of a nation which basically was the child of Yahweh, preoccupied with its problems and troubles, which looked to him to protect the people and to keep them safe from harm in order that they could survive, and the idea of a nation called by Yahweh to take up again the basic purpose for which the nation had come into existence. These were difficult times, and both viewpoints contributed to the ongoing religious development. But these were not the only religious developments that were taking place. There were two other movements that were part of this milieu and which contributed much to the religious thinking of the times and would have greater significance for the future.

The first of these was the flowering of the Wisdom movement. This movement found its way into Israelite thought at a later time than many of the other nations surrounding her. Babylonia and Egypt had flourishing Wisdom traditions very early, but it was probably only later in the court of Solomon that the Wisdom movement received its momentum in Israel. "Wisdom" differs in some ways from the other Old Testament writings in that it tends to be more international in flavor and individual in character, and it probably began as a "secular" movement almost everywhere. The intent of the wise man was to enable persons to live at peace and in harmony and prosperity in this world. It basically was a prudential ethic that taught people to obey the "rules" of the world so that all would be well in one's life. It was, as one can readily see, quite similar in basic philosophy to the Deuteronomic theory of life.

But, as with everything else Israel appropriated from her neighbors and culture, wisdom too was invested with the basic religion of Yahweh. "The fear of Yahweh is the beginning of wisdom" (cf. Prov. 1:7; Job 28:28). The rules of the world were made by Yahweh and should be obeyed not simply because this would mean a better life but because Yahweh expected such conduct from his people.

Most Wisdom movements were characterized by two distinct types. The first is the most obvious, namely, the practical or *prudential* type, wherein the student is informed that X produces Y and that X is to be either adhered to zealously or shunned totally (cf. Proverbs 10:1–22:16 especially). The second type is *speculative,* "philosophical," in that the writer is attempting to explore the deeper meanings of life and the inconsistencies that are part of this world. It simply is *not* true that the good are rewarded always and the evil punished. It is not true that the good do not suffer unjustly. The practical wisdom explained this phenomenon as a chastening to bring about a better reward or way of life. But if one is honest, it can be readily seen that life is not that simple! Why then all the unjust suffering in the world? How is it to be explained? The speculative wisdom writers wrestled with these problems.

The books of the Old Testament which belong basically to this latter type are Job and Ecclesiastes, and it was in these books that the old Deuteronomic ideas began to be questioned. The book of Job (which may be a drama) concerned a righteous man whose faith was put to the test. Many interpreters of Job view the central theme as the question of why must the righteous suffer, or the problem of theodicy, God's justice, or why does God allow such things to happen in his world. But these questions were never answered and were really left unexplained. The author of the book of Job explained the situation in accordance with the basics of biblical religion. After Job argued with his three "friends" (chs. 3–31), Yahweh spoke to Job out of the whirlwind (38–41). He never answered Job's questions; he merely revealed himself in his splendor, wonder, and majesty. And it was then that Job learned the hard lesson that the important thing in this world is whether one "knows" this God and is in the proper relationship with him. All other aspects of life are secondary. The book itself is full of the pathos and paradoxes of human existence—the wronged sufferer who is in agony and yet becomes insufferable; the friends who have all the answers to life neatly catalogued ready to apply them; the person who wants to give up (Job's wife); and the person who feels that everyone is wrong but adds nothing to the situation (Elihu, chapters 32–37).

Job challenged God to answer him, and after he did Job can only say:

> I had heard of you by the hearing of the ear,
> but now my eye sees you;
> therefore I despise myself,
> and repent in dust and ashes. (42:5–6, paraphrase)

This central point of this marvelous piece of literature has been summarized excellently: "The poem of Job ends on a central biblical truth: if God is to be known he must make Himself known and no amount of talking about Him can replace the reality of His presence or the void of His absence. . . . As for the purpose of suffering, the book of Job offers several suggestions but no dogma. Suffering may be retribution, testing, discipline, or it may in the end be largely inexplicable. What matters is the purity of one's relation with God, unadulterated by the circumstances of success or failure."[4]

The second speculative wisdom book is called Ecclesiastes. This work revolves around struggles of a person, called Koheleth (the Preacher), who sought to find the meaning and purpose of life. He looked for fulfillment and purpose in knowledge, pleasure, work, power, but found nothing except an emptiness. "Behold all is vanity and a striving after the wind" (1:14b *et al.*). The author was indeed a pessimistic person, skeptical about whether the world is in order, has any meaning, or is worth the effort! But too many interpreters have missed the very positive point which the author made in the midst of all the negative ones. Koheleth believed that life *is* worth the effort, and in spite of everything "where there's life, there's hope!" "But he who is joined with all the living has hope, for a living dog is better than a dead lion." (9:4)

The book of Ecclesiastes is another of those books which almost was excluded from the Old Testament canon. It was "saved" by the final editor's addition which gave a more positive note to the work (12:9–14). But the message of the book stands on its own. Men cannot understand the mysteries of life; wisdom *per se* is not the salvation of the world (cf. 8:16–17). The ultimate meaning and purpose is beyond us, but humanity must do the best it can and find as much happiness as possible. Otherwise life can be a real bore!

The greatness of both Job and Ecclesiastes perhaps lies at least in part in that the authors wrestle with these thorny problems of life, but without any thought of a life hereafter which will make all things "even" again. In spite of the fact that the Deuteronomic philosophy of life was now being severely questioned because it was not "realistic," there was not yet any development into a doctrine of life after death with rewards and punishments. Job asked "If a man die, will he live again?" (14:14). The answer, of course, was *no*. Koheleth said, ". . . one fate comes to all, to the righteous and the wicked, to the good and the evil, to the clean and the unclean, to him who sacrifices and him who does not sacrifice" (9:2a). It may well be that these thinkers opened the way for further development and thought about that matter which did indeed take place later.

It was indicated previously that there were two other developments in the post-exilic period in addition to the prevailing moods of exclusivism and the opposing reactions. One was wisdom, which has now been examined in brief. The second, apocalyptic, must be set in the larger historical situation.

Additional Readings

Bible: Ezra 1; Nehemiah 8–9, 13; Jonah; Ruth; Esther; Job; Ecclesiastes

Secondary Material:

Wood, James. *Wisdom Literature: An Introduction.* London: Gerald Duckworth & Co., Ltd., 1967.

Scott, R. B. Y. *The Way of Wisdom in the Old Testament.* New York: The Macmillan Co., 1971.

Murphy, Roland E. *Seven Books of Wisdom.* Milwaukee: Bruce Publishing Co., 1960.

Ringgren, Helmer. *The Faith of the Psalmists.* London: SCM Press, 1963.

Eaton, J. H. *Psalms: Introduction and Commentary.* Torch Bible Commentary Series. London: SCM Press, 1967.

Ackroyd, Peter R. *Israel Under Babylon and Persia.* The New Clarendon Bible, Old Testament, Vol. IV. London: Oxford University Press, 1970.

Myers, J. M. *The World of the Restoration.* Backgrounds to the Bible Series. Englewood Cliffs, N. J.: Prentice-Hall, Inc., 1968.

Snaith, N. H. *The Jews From Cyrus to Herod.* New York: Abingdon-Cokesbury Press, 1956, pp. 7–30.

Notes Chapter 5

1. The evidence is even more conclusive when one reads in the texts that the high priest when Nehemiah served was Eliashib, but the high priest when Ezra served was Eliashib's grandson, Jehohanan!

2. Whether this book was the Torah as we now know it or part of it, we do not know, but this document did become the basis for the religion of the community.

3. This book purports to explain the origin of the Feast of Purim, a very popular feast in terms of idea and practice among the Jews of the post-exilic period. This probably explains how it was admitted into the canon since God is never mentioned in this work!

4. N.K. Gottwald, *A Light to the Nations* (New York: Harper & Row, 1959), p. 485.

6
The Hellenistic Period and the Rise of Apocalyptic

The post-exilic period for the people in Judah was one of confusion, frustration, and searching. The memories of the exile, the establishment of the new community centered in the Temple, and the struggle for survival were all "givens" of their situation. But these people were only part of a much larger scene over which they had little or no control and which added to their confusion in their search for meaning.

After Alexander the Great had made his lightning conquests (332–323 B. C.), that part of the world could no longer be the same. Alexander had a dream of world empire based on a common culture (basically Greek), and wherever he could he imposed Greek ideas on the conquered peoples, a process known as Hellenization. His untimely death in 323 B. C. led to a long series of wars among his generals for control over the areas already conquered. When the smoke of the battles had finally cleared in 301 B. C., his kingdom had been divided into four basic units. The two which influenced Palestine were the Seleucid rule (Persia and Palestine to Phoenicia) and the Ptolemaic rule (Egypt and Southern Palestine). Because of its proximity to both, the area where the Jews lived was a disputed territory for a long time.

At first Judah was under the control of the Ptolemies, who did not really push the Hellenization program of Alexander. Religiously speaking, the Ptolemies left that almost entirely to the Jews themselves. But in 198 B. C., after another in a long series of fierce battles, the Ptolemies simply gave up attempting to keep this area, and Judah fell under the rule of the Seleucids.

During this period (i.e., down to ca. 200 B. C.) the Jews in Palestine were having extremely hard times. Economically they were in such dire circumstances that Egypt exacted no taxes from them, and the Syrians granted them a three-year respite from any taxes when they assumed control.

Ideologically the period was one where many philosophies and thought patterns were being espoused and examined. Persian thought and Greek thought, along with the Oriental thought patterns, were being blended and to a certain degree assimilated into the thinking of the people. New customs were being introduced and to a limited degree adopted, thus challenging some of the older ways and thinking. Also during this period many Jews moved away from Palestine, especially to larger cities such as Alexandria in Egypt. These people were exposed even more to other cultures, customs, and philosophies.

It also became necessary, because of this dispersion, to translate the Hebrew Torah into a language which these people could understand. Thus in the third century B. C. the Torah was translated into Greek at Alexandria, and this Greek translation is called the *Septuagint.* In spite of the increasing dispersion of the Jews, however, the center for Judaism remained in Jerusalem in the Temple.

It is here that we can pick up the history once again. In 175 B. C. the Seleucid ruler, Antiochus IV, accepted a bribe from the current High Priest's brother that he be appointed High Priest. The High Priest was not only the religious leader of the Jews but held much political power as well. Having accepted the bribe, Antiochus deposed the current office holder, Onias III, and appointed his brother Joshua as High Priest. This move not only gave Antiochus money, but it gave him more political power over the people as well. The process of Hellenization had not developed significantly among the Jews, and it was Joshua's duty to see that it did.

Changing his name to Jason (the Greek equivalent), Joshua pushed aspects of Greek culture such as dress, manners, games, etc. But in 171 Jason was outbid for the office by a certain Menelaus; while Jason was not looked upon as the *legitimate* High Priest by the people, he was at least a member of the priestly family. Menelaus, however,

was not, and trouble flared. Jason deposed Menelaus, who appealed
to Antiochus for help. Antiochus came to the rescue and placed
Menelaus in office again by force.

Trouble and unrest continued so that Antiochus, rightly understanding that the basic cause of the discontent was rooted in the
religion of these people, outlawed the Jewish religion. It was declared
a capital offense to circumcise children, to have a copy of the Torah,
or even to keep the Sabbath. To add insult to injury, he declared the
Temple in Jerusalem sacred to Zeus, erected a statue of Zeus there,
and even sacrificed pigs on the altar! This occurred in December,
168/7.

Not long after these events an old priest of Yahweh named Mat-
tathias killed a Syrian soldier who was enforcing the worship of Zeus
and with his sons retreated into the hill country to wage guerilla
warfare against the Syrians. He died in 166 but commissioned his son,
Judas, to lead the war for freedom.[1] Some readily joined in the fight,
but others were more skeptical. The most notable of these latter was
a group known as the *Hasidim* ("Pious Ones") who wanted religious
freedom but were reluctant to fight. This changed when on a Sabbath
the Syrians found a large group of Hasidim hiding in a cave and
slaughtered them. Since it was the Sabbath, the group offered no
opposition. After this episode, however, the Hasidim joined in the
fight, and in 165/4 Judas won a victory over the Syrian army in the
area. The proscription against Judaism was lifted, and the Temple was
reconsecrated and rededicated in December, 165/4. This is still celebrated as the Feast of Hanukkah or the Feast of Lights.

After this the Hasidim ceased to be a part of the resistance movement, religious freedom having been won, but the Maccabees continued to fight hoping for political freedom and power. By 141 B. C.
they had won a degree of political independence, and the dynasty
(known as the Hasmonean dynasty) was inaugurated. This dynasty of
priest-kings remained in power till 63 B. C., when for all practical
purposes political independence for this area was over. It was in 63
that Pompey, the great Roman general, captured this part of the
world for Rome. The area was later ruled by Herod the Great (an
Idumean, i.e., Edomite) under Roman authority. And when Herod
died (4 B. C.), the land was parcelled out among his three sons, with

Judah soon after (6 A. D.) becoming a Roman province under a Roman governor.

It was in such a setting that a new religious emphasis developed, the apocalyptic.

Apocalyptic literature is a special type of literary genre, just as is poetry, drama, and the like. The roots of this type of thinking go back to Persia and had been known to the Jewish people for some time. Culturally speaking this literature was most prevalent in periods of persecution and hard times. It is not difficult to understand why this type of movement would develop in Judah during this portion of history.

Apocalyptic writing and thought have numerous characteristics which need careful attention, since this particular type of literary genre seems strange and far-removed from the thought patterns of the twentieth century. There are two primary characteristics of apocalyptic thought and literature and numerous secondary characteristics which demand clarification.[2] The two primary characteristics are (1) dualism, and (2) eschatology. Persian thought held as a common belief that there was going on at a cosmic level a life and death struggle between the forces of good and evil and that this struggle intruded itself into this world order. There is in this created order a dualism between good and evil, light and darkness. Exactly how directly this Persian thought affected the religious thinking of the post-exilic community is not known, but it is clear that this type of thought pattern is one of the foci for apocalyptic ideology.

The other focus centers in the idea that history is divided into two ages: (1) a present evil age under the immediate dominion of the forces of evil in which the righteous are persecuted; and (2) a coming age which will be established after God intervenes and destroys evil, thus removing the persecution, and inaugurates a period of happiness. This is the basic eschatological (i.e., ideas concerning the "end") emphasis of apocalyptic thinking. Because of the highly poetic nature of this literary genre there is little consistency among the apocalyptic writers as to exactly how God's intervention was to take place or exactly what kind of new age was to be established. Some felt it was to be a transformed earth, some a supra-historical order within the time process yet above it, and others a completely new life somewhere in a "spiritual" existence. Whatever the exact nature of the new age, it would be a time when evil was subdued, good exalted, and the persecution gone.

In addition to these two basic ideas there are numerous secondary characteristics as well which distinguish most but not *all* apocalyptic works. The first is that the person who is writing claims to have "seen" the events he reports in a vision, and the vision is unusual and bizarre, which necessitates someone, usually an angel, to explain the meaning to the "seer." This "seer" is ordinarily some ancient worthy of the past such as Abraham, Moses, Ezra, Baruch, etc. In other words, most apocalyptic writings are pseudonymous. Consequently the work has a tendency to be "deterministic," i.e., human history is "fixed" in such a way that events will run their course as they are supposed to. This device was utilized by the apocalyptic writers to engender hope, for if the bad things "predicted" had come to pass, surely the good would also.

The vision seen by the "ancient" writer would depict with highly symbolic images the history of the people of God (and others related to them) down to the circumstances of history in which the people of God were presently experiencing persecution for their faith. If the persecution which was "predicted" has indeed come to pass, then the judgment on the old age and the removal of the persecution of God's people will surely occur also as the apocalyptic writer predicts. There is, then, in most all apocalyptic works a long section outlining history up to the present by means of weird symbolism and imagery.

The apocalyptic writers, naturally poetic and obviously highly imaginative persons, utilized this symbolism with gusto! Beasts of all shapes and descriptions abound, usually symbolizing nations or rulers who exercise and execute power. A horn symbolizes power or someone who exercises power. Judgment scenes are made more dramatic and awesome by the use of unusual natural phenomena such as earthquakes, eclipses, falling stars, and the like. Numbers too play an important part in apocalyptic symbolism. Three is the number dealing with the spirit world; four with the created order; seven is the perfect (sometimes the "complete") number; ten is the usual number indicating completeness; twelve is the number symbolizing the "people of God"; and three and one-half is the number which indicates the allotted time for the reign of evil which is perpetrating the persecution of God's people. This evil must run its course but will surely come to an end and receive its just deserts. Colors also play a part in the symbolism: white usually depicting victory; red, war; black, plague or pestilence; green, eternity; "pale" or greenish-yellow, death.

Most commentators on the apocalyptic movement also find a pessimism in this literature which extends beyond the present age of persecution and denies any hope for the historical order whatsoever. The world order as we know it must be destroyed and some new "spiritual existence" must take the place of life as we understand it now. It is true that some apocalyptic writers do indeed feel this way about the present world,[3] but the two biblical apocalypses (Daniel and Revelation) are not that pessimistic about human history. To be sure, the present age is an evil one and must be destroyed or rather transformed, but the new age in both takes place in a transformed human society within the historical process. Therefore, while it is true that some extra-biblical apocalyptic works despair of human history and this created order, the biblical apocalyptic works do not.

Another characteristic of apocalyptic works was the belief in angels and demons. Because of the great struggle between the forces of good and evil which takes place at a cosmic level, there are beings who fight in that sphere. During the post-exilic age there developed not only the belief in angels and demons but in hierarchies of angels and demons. And it must be pointed out that this and many features of apocalyptic literature were so popular that much apocalyptic thinking permeated the religious thinking of the period even in writings which were not apocalyptic *per se*.

It is now appropriate to examine perhaps the last book written which was included in the canon of the Old Testament. The Book of Daniel is a work that is composed of two parts: (1) a series of stories about Daniel and his friends in exile in Babylon; and (2) a series of apocalyptic visions revealed to Daniel. Scholars are generally agreed that the book was written in the Maccabean period, ca. 165 B. C. One can date apocalyptic works partly at least by observing when in the book the "history" stops being correct and begins to "miss the mark." It is probably at that point that the book was written. (In Daniel this comes specifically in chapter 11 when the author misses the time and place of Antiochus' death.)

As one reads the book it is easy to see how the episodes and visions would speak to the people under the persecution of Antiochus. The story in chapter one dealing with food, in chapter three dealing with worshiping an image, and in chapter six dealing with proper prayer and worship even when it is expressly forbidden are all related to and directed at the program of persecution under Antiochus IV. The promise in chapter two is that the new age would come after the Babylonian, Median, Persian, and Greek empires had exercised authority and power for their allotted time. Chapter four shows that God judges men who exalt themselves as gods; and chapter five announces the judgment on Babylon for treating the true God with contempt and disrespect.

The apocalyptic visions give much the same picture with chapter seven paralleling chapter two. Chapters eight through eleven give the historical survey in typical apocalyptic imagery. All this leads to the climax in chapter twelve, which unfortunately has been often misunderstood. There is here the typical apocalyptic motif of the end of the age (*not* the end of time) when the persecution is completed, and God's elect live free from the torment of the oppressors. The author of Daniel inserts a unique motif, the idea of resurrection (12:1f.). This is a physical resurrection to life *in this world*. It is, however, only a partial resurrection, "some" being raised to life and "some" to shame. There are various attempts to explain the passage, but it seems clear that the resurrection here is for those who have been martyred in the persecution and who will be raised to receive their just reward; and for those who have inflicted evil on God's elect who will be raised to receive their just punishment. The implication seems to be that after the scales have been balanced, the persons involved will return to Sheol.[4]

One other motif should be considered here in connection with apocalyptic. It is often believed that the weird symbolism and imagery were employed by the writers because they did not want their persecutors to understand the writing; in short, apocalyptic was a form of cryptogram. As widely accepted as this tenet is, it does not seem to fit the facts. In almost every case when the "seer" observes a vision beset with wild images, the whole scene is clearly explained by the angel who accompanies him (cf. Daniel 7–11). Now unless it is assumed that the persecutors could not read or were completely ignorant, it is difficult to ascertain how the meaning could not be known to the oppressor. It seems more in line with the literary genre and the historical circumstances to understand the symbolism as part of the literary type. Persecution is a horrible and hideous spectre; it must be described in terms appropriate to gauge its intensity. And the intensity of the evil that lies behind persecution must be dwarfed by the intensity of the righteousness and power of the One who is about to destroy it! The fact is that the oppressors did not take these writings very seriously; such writings were probably viewed by them as "grasping at straws" by persons who could not possibly be a threat to them. And if these oppressed people wanted to believe that their God was going to act on their behalf, that was fine! Perhaps it would even make them more submissive.

With Daniel one comes to the end of the Old Testament canon. Much thinking takes place between the Book of Daniel and the episodes about which we read in the Gospels of the New Testament. We can learn much about this development by examining the books of the Apocrypha and Pseudepigrapha.[5] The term Apocrypha is used for those books found in the Greek translations of the Old Testament but which were not admitted into the Hebrew canon, and the broader term Pseudepigrapha at one time included almost everything else. Since the designation of these terms other literature has been found (i.e., the Dead Sea Scrolls). It is not our purpose here to enumerate or outline this great body of literature, but some of the religious ideas developed and depicted in them must be examined so that the religious milieu presupposed by the New Testament writers will not seem strange. The writings of the "Intertestamental" period range all the way from history writing to religious fiction. And *many* religious ideas and motifs were evolving. It would be impossible to enumerate them all but several do deserve special mention.

Theology *per se,* i.e., the thinking about God, had pushed God further and further away from his created order, and therefore from intimate relationship with humanity. More and more he was viewed as a transcendent being whose only contact with the world came through mediators. This type of thought, coupled with the growing emphasis upon angels and demons in apocalyptic, naturally aided in the developing interest in angels as mediators of revelation. It was even felt that the Law (the Torah) had been given to Moses not directly but through angel mediators.

There was, further, an interest in the origin of Sin. Some found the source of Sin to have originated in the fall of Adam and Eve; in this line of thought it was usually felt that the entire human race fell when Adam fell (cf. corporate personality motif). Others argued that sin was "imported" into human experience completely from outside, even originating with the Devil.[6] Still others argued that human nature, while not sinful in itself, was weak and frail and susceptible to the strong powers of the forces of evil which overpower all persons. The rabbis developed a quite similar idea involving "impulses." Human beings are born with two "impulses" or "inclinations" (called a *yetzer*); one of these inclines toward good, the *yetzer ha-tob,* and one inclines toward evil, the *yetzer ha-ra'.* Life is a constant struggle to do the good, to allow the *yetzer ha-tob* to grow and gain command over one's life and to subdue the *yetzer ha-ra'.*

Partly because of the questioning by the speculative wing of the Wisdom movement of the Deuteronomic ideas, partly because of new ideas from other philosophies in the world, partly because of the new emphasis on suffering and the apocalyptic ideas about the two ages, and partly because of further thinking about life and death, etc., there was a tremendous amount of speculation during this period in the area of eschatology. There were those who still basically adhered to the concept of Sheol; others believed in a day of resurrection when judgment would be rendered on good and evil—and persons individually would be rewarded or punished according to their deeds. What happened between death and the day of judgment was also debated. Some believed in a type of "soul sleep"; others thought that persons would remain in Sheol until the time of judgment; others believed in a type of intermediate state where proleptically one began to experience some of the joys or sorrows which awaited them later; while others believed that the reward or punishment began immediately upon death. Some believed in a type of immortality, while others believed in a physical resurrection from the dead, sometimes to life in this world, sometimes to life in another realm after the Judgment. As is evident, there was much ferment taking place in this important area of religious ideology, but there was no real consistency or unanimity of opinion about the matter.

The same is true of the concept of Messiah. Some writers still looked forward to a Messianic Age with God ruling over all without any Messiah as such. There were others who because of the historical circumstance of the Hasmonean dynasty looked again for a Messiah. To some he would be a political type of the line of David; to others a priestly type like the Hasmoneans; to some he was an earthly human character, while others depicted him as a divine or semi-divine being. The growth in popularity of apocalyptic coupled with certain ideas about a Messiah produced in this period a belief known as the "Messianic Woes." This teaching held that when the Messiah did come that there would be associated with that event (perhaps before, perhaps after) a period of intense suffering which would be shared by the Messiah and the people of God. This was quite in keeping with the idea of the apocalyptic writers that this present age was evil, that evil had to run its course, and the greatest concentration of evil would come at the time immediately before the intervention of God on behalf of his people. It was, therefore, this period of great trial and tribulation that was associated with the coming of the Messiah and designated the "Messianic Woes."

The list of religious motifs and ideas which were being debated and in which there was intense struggle to find meaning during this period could be expounded almost indefinitely. To say that there was one specific set of ideas that held the primary attention of the people would be to ignore the vast number of writings with their varied and diverse ideas and emphases. It was a time of intense searching and struggle when "growing pains" abounded, religiously speaking. Politically the people looked for someone or something to release them from the yoke of foreign oppression. They believed intensely that God was going to act on their behalf. Exactly how or by what means or when was unknown to them. It was in this type of setting that the events recorded in the Gospels transpired.

Additional Reading

Bible: Daniel

Secondary Material:

Snaith, N. H. *The Jews From Cyrus to Herod,* pp. 31–203.

Rowley, H. H. *The Relevance of Apocalyptic,* 3rd rev. ed. New York: Association Press, 1963.

Russell, D. S. *The Method and Message of Jewish Apocalyptic: 200 B. C.–A. D. 100.* Philadelphia: The Westminster Press, 1964.

Schmithals, Walter. *The Apocalyptic Movement: Introduction and Interpretation.* Trans. by J. E. Steely. New York: Abingdon Press, 1975.

Charles, R. H. *Religious Development Between the Old and New Testaments.* New York: H. Holt & Co., 1914.

_____. *Eschatology: The Doctrine of a Future Life in Israel, Judaism and Christianity.* Introduction by G. W. Buchanan. New York: Shocken Books, Inc., 1963. (Original edition 1899.)

Porteous, N. W. *Daniel: A Commentary.* The Old Testament Library. Philadelphia: Westminster Press, 1965.

Notes Chapter 6

1. It is this Judas who became known as Maccabaeus, "Hammer," and from this title comes the designation for this period of Jewish history, the Maccabaean era.

2. These characteristics are basically outlined in Martin Rist, "Apocalyptic," in *The Interpreter's Dictionary of the Bible,* Vol. I, pp. 157–61.

3. For examination of some extra-canonical apocalyptic literature, cf. R.H. Charles, *The Apocrypha and Pseudepigrapha of the Old Testament* (London: Oxford University Press, 1913), 2 Vols.; cf. Vol. II.

4. The word often translated "eternal" or "everlasting" in this passage basically means "age," i.e., life in the new age which will restore equity to the order of God's justice. The Deuteronomic philosophy did not go away easily!

5. Cf. R. H. Charles, *op. cit.,* footnote 3.

6. It was during this period that the idea of a being who led the forces of evil developed. Known by various names in the different books, he became known basically as the Devil and was connected with the Old Testament figure of Satan. Whatever his name, his power was great and he ruled over a large kingdom of demons and exercised tremendous influence in the universe, even invading and corrupting human history.

7
New Testament Background and the Synoptic Gospels

At the conclusion of the preceding chapter it was clearly seen just how diverse the religious ideas of this period were. The makeup of the overall political situation was diverse as well, but *one* thing was certain politically speaking—Rome ruled! And it was under the yoke of Rome that the Jewish people chafed. They looked forward to a time when that hated tyranny would be overthrown and the Kingdom (their Kingdom) established.

That, of course, was the view from the Jewish standpoint. From the Roman standpoint it looked different. After all, the people there had relative peace now; they had no reason to fear a change of rulers every several years. In practical terms, the Romans were lenient rulers and tried to interfere in the life of the conquered people as little as possible. But one fact remained: Palestine was the frontier of the Empire in this part of the world, a buffer state dividing the Roman Empire from the recently revived Persian Empire now called Parthia. It was of utmost importance to Rome to keep peace in the frontier because the slightest sign of uprising against Rome would invite invasion. Therefore any kind of political unrest had to be dealt with quickly and efficiently.

As far as religious organization was concerned, there were several quasi-religious "parties" which emerged in Judaism at this time and were influential in various ways. The most important of these was the Pharisees. It is believed that this group emerged out of the *Hasidim* of the Maccabean era. These persons did not attempt to dabble in politics any more than absolutely necessary; they were more interested in religious matters. "Doctrinally" they held that God directed the affairs of mankind—but in such a way as *not* to interfere with or infringe upon the freedom and responsibility of human beings. These people believed in a life after death with a resurrection to reward and punishment, and also believed in angels and demons. The authority of the Torah was strictly upheld, but in addition they accepted the oral traditions which had been passed down relating to the interpretation of the Torah.[1] It was from this group in all probability that the scribes were drawn. The Pharisees then were very influential, were connected primarily with the Synagogue and the interpretation of the written Scriptures, and were composed basically of lay persons, not the priests.

A second group composed primarily of priests was the Sadducees. This group adhered most closely to the written Torah, rejecting the oral traditions. They dismissed the idea of any resurrection, any doctrine of a Messiah, the belief in angels and demons, and they believed that people have the freedom to choose to do good or evil and that each person is responsible for the decisions made! Being priests, these persons naturally were quite involved with the Temple and its cultus, and it is not surprising then that after 70 A. D. we hear of them no more.[2]

Another group is called the Essenes. These people believed in separating themselves from the evil society around them. Some moved into communities (with rigorous rules and regulations), usually far away from settled cities and communities. The Dead Sea Scroll community (Qumran) was evidently one of these groups. Some others lived apart but did "missionary" work among the people of their world. Most of these groups emphasized religious and ceremonial purity and looked for the establishment of the Kingdom of the righteous at any time.

Josephus called the next group the "Fourth Philosophy." They are usually known as Zealots. Here were persons cut from the cloth of the Maccabean period and inspired by zeal for Jewish purity, independence, and political power. Most of these people really believed that open war with Rome was the answer to their problems. "If we begin a war with Rome, then God will be obligated to intervene on our behalf, and thus the kingdom will be established. So, why wait?" There was an even more fanatical group within the Zealot ranks who practiced assassination of Romans and/or Roman sympathizers. These people were called *Sicarii,* which comes from the Latin for "dagger."[3]

Lest one receive the wrong idea about these "parties," it would be well to point out that these groups were not highly organized, close-knit factions, but rather loosely connected groups of persons who generally held similar beliefs. It is probable that fewer than ten per cent of the population belonged to one of these "parties."

The vast majority of the people belonged to the segment of society known as the *amme-ha-arets,* "the people of the land." These were the ordinary hard working people who had little time for religious niceties and philosophical discourses. They were too busy trying to eke out a basic existence. They did not know all the minutiae of the Torah (and probably did not want to know them) but were nominally religious. It was these people with whom Jesus worked and lived. And it was these people who were probably filled with apocalyptic expectations.

Whereas the Old Testament centers in the Exodus, the New Testament centers in the Person of Jesus of Nazareth. According to the New Testament teaching, the *kerygma,* Jesus is the central focus of a great event accomplished by the power of God on behalf of humanity. The records that we have in the New Testament, as in the Old Testament, do not make claim to be objective, non-interpreted accounts of what really happened. It was their purpose to proclaim what was their belief that God had acted mightily on their behalf in and through the life and ministry of Jesus. The Gospels, then, are not really biographical accounts (even though they *contain* biographical materials), but rather proclamations, "good news," about the new "thing" that God had done on behalf of the world.

The Gospels are four separate accounts or "portraits" of Jesus. Each one should be read and studied separately in order to understand what each writer had to say about this Jesus. Before turning to an examination of the three Synoptic Gospels individually, it is necessary for the interpreter to be aware of some of the basic types of approach to the study of these documents which are prevalent in New Testament studies. One of these approaches deals with the period before any of the stories and sayings were written down but were passed along in oral form. This discipline is called *form-criticism*. The assumption of this study is that the earliest records of Jesus' life and teaching were transmitted orally, and that in the process of transmission certain "forms" evolved to facilitate the transmission of the tradition.[4] According to some experts in this area of research the stories were remembered and shaped by the needs of the early Christian community so much so that what we have in the Gospels is little more than a reflection of the thinking of the early Church.

This kind of reasoning has led in some quarters to a sharp distinction being drawn between the "Jesus of history" (i.e., Jesus as he "really" was) and the "Christ of faith" (i.e., the proclaimed Lord of the early Church). The student of the Bible should keep in mind that this is a distinction that modern scholars make but no such dichotomy would be drawn in the minds of the early Christians. These two emphases which some present scholarship tends to dissect were to them inseparable. As in the Old Testament it was not simply an event that was important; it was the event *plus* the interpretation of that event. Neither of these two ingredients is dispensable to the biblical mode of thought.

Form-criticism is a very useful method and helps in interpretation at numerous points. It is limited, however, in its usefulness in interpreting the Gospels, since it is by its nature more analytical than synthetic, but the discipline has made us acutely aware of the setting of these writings in the context of the early Church and its needs.

Another approach is to be found in *source-criticism*. This area of study concentrates on the Gospels themselves and attempts to analyze as much as one can the basic sources out of which the Gospels were composed. This particular method has been exceedingly helpful especially at the point of offering a solution to the "Synoptic problem." Briefly put, the Synoptic problem consists in the similarities and dissimilarities among Matthew, Mark, and Luke. Why are these three so much alike? Why are they different? The solution that is generally accepted is that Mark was the earliest written Gospel and was used by both Matthew and Luke in the composition of their Gospels. The outlines are similar, and when one deviates from the pattern it is always Mark that is the common denominator both in terms of outline and content.

There is, however, a large amount of material in Matthew and Luke that is not found in Mark. Some of this material is common to both Matthew and Luke and consists basically in teachings of Jesus. Therefore there is postulated a "sayings source" containing a collection of Jesus' teachings used by both Matthew and Luke in the composition of their Gospels. This source is designated by the symbol Q (from the German *Quelle,* source). But when the Markan material and the Q material have been extracted from Matthew and Luke, there is still left in each of these Gospels a large amount of material peculiar to each. That material which has been left is designated as M (for that special to Matthew) and L (that special to Luke). These sources may have been written, but it is more probable that the materials were both oral and written, available to the authors of these Gospels to be used according to the purposes and designs they wanted to espouse.

This leads us to the third of the methods employed in studying the Gospels, the method known as *redaction-criticism.* This discipline attempts to emphasize the basic message of the book as a whole literary unity. The questions this approach attempts to answer are those that deal with the religious emphases and message of the book, and the portrait of Jesus depicted in the writing. The idea here is that no matter what the history of the form or the written source may have been, the selection of the data, the writing, editing, and arrangement of each Gospel have been produced by each author for specific reasons, and each Gospel should be studied as an entity and unity to itself. There was a wealth of information available to the Gospel writers, both oral and written. What they did with this material has been preserved for us as the Gospels of Mark, Matthew, and Luke.

Mark

When critical scholarship first began its very fruitful researches on the Synoptic problem, it was discovered that Mark was the oldest of all. It was also felt that Mark was closest to the "historical Jesus." Matthew and Luke followed Mark, to be sure, but they and John had placed theological layers over the Jesus of history. Mark, however, had not, or had done so in such a way that there was a minimal amount of theology. His was basically a historical, factual account of Jesus' life and ministry.

Upon closer examination of the text itself, however, Mark was found to be a highly theological document. It is not simply a "human Jesus" that he depicts but the one who was "Son of God" in a unique way as well! Jesus' entire life is spent proclaiming the Kingdom of God (which had begun in his ministry) and demonstrating that the Kingdom had in fact been inaugurated by his mastery over the demons, representatives of the Kingdom of Satan. He constantly challenged the people by his parables to choose between the Kingdom of God and the Kingdom of Satan whose powers presently enslave them. The baptism scene in 1:10–11 was interpreted by Mark to demonstrate Jesus' special kinship with God as well as the transfiguration scene (9:2–8) and the parable or allegory about the vineyard (12).

Another theme that Mark emphasizes is that of suffering. Jesus is a suffering Messiah. Throughout the Gospel, beginning with the baptismal scene, Jesus is depicted as Messiah, but as a Messiah who must suffer to accomplish his goals. In writing to a church that had just experienced persecution, the author emphasizes Jesus' suffering and his troubles with those in authority as a way of bolstering the spirits of those in the church and encouraging them in their struggles.

There is yet one feature of Mark's gospel that still puzzles New Testament scholars, that is, his emphasis upon secrecy.[5] Jesus constantly invoked persons (with one exception in 5:1f.) to remain silent about him. He refused to allow the demons to identify him; Mark even interpreted Jesus' use of parables (one of the simplest and easiest ways to be understood!) as a means whereby the people would *not* be able to recognize him (cf. 4:10–12).[6] The problem of exactly what the secret was and how this idea developed is still not solved.

One of the reasons for this may be owing to the fact that the original ending of Mark has been lost. The oldest and best Greek texts conclude with 16:8, which does not seem to be a complete sentence, let alone an ending for the Gospel. This is especially demonstrated in that Mark indicated there would be appearances of the risen Jesus in Galilee, but none are given.

Mark's gospel is characterized by a rough and vivid style which is well suited to Mark's portrait of Jesus as a man of action. The basic emphasis is upon Jesus as the "announcer" and bringer of the Kingdom of God. He is a man of action in mortal conflict with the Kingdom of Satan. God's Kingdom has been inaugurated with his ministry, but will be finally consummated in the future. There is a realism in this account that is missing in the others, however. Jesus is hungry, tired, angry, sad, and surprised. The necessity of the cross looms large in Mark's account, since Mark roots Jesus' ministry in the concept of the suffering servant motif of Isaiah 40–55. The death of Jesus is viewed as a ransom for other people (cf. especially Isaiah 52:13–53:12); He is a "Servant-Messiah." And the resurrection is looked forward to as the validation by God on Jesus' messianic life.

Matthew

The Gospel of Matthew has been long a favorite among those who study the life and especially the teaching of Jesus. It was written in Palestine 80–100 A. D. (probably the later date is closer) to serve as a manual of instruction in the Church or as a polemical guide in the "evangelization" of the Jews. That the former could be the case is seen in the author's methodology, which is to collect and arrange the teaching of Jesus (scattered throughout Mark and Q in Luke) into "discourses" or sermons. There are at least five of these, perhaps six (5–7, 10, 13, 18, 24–25, probably also 23).

But the emphasis in Matthew is so overwhelmingly slanted toward the Church's relationship to the Jewish people that it is difficult to find anything other than a work designed to be used as a way of dealing with the problem of how the Christian Church is to relate to the Jewish people. This was a real problem because the early Church (and Paul) viewed the Christian movement as nothing less than God's continuation of his covenant ties with his special people which covenant went all the way back to Abraham and Moses. They believed that the Israel of God was not interrupted but that the new Israel was the Christian Church, not the Jewish nation! Matthew's Gospel emphasized that Jesus is the Messiah and the fulfillment of "true Judaism." This explains the inordinate emphasis in Matthew on "proving" that Jesus is Messiah by appeal to Old Testament passages.

It is a benefit to any student to understand the manner in which the New Testament writers used the Old Testament Scriptures (the Old Testament being the *only* Bible of the New Testament Church!). The method employed was similar in many respects to the ways the Rabbinic schools interpreted the sacred writings. The method goes something like this: the early Church or Christian writer knew of an historical event (or they thought the event was historical). In reading the Old Testament, they then could find verses that seemed to fit the historical situation; whether it had anything to do with the original meaning was probably not considered. But the historical event was then viewed as being the fulfillment of the Old Testament passage.

For example, in Matthew 2:15 the author viewed the historical occurrence, the flight of the family into Egypt, and interpreted Hosea 11:1, "Out of Egypt have I called my son," (a reference in Hosea to the Exodus) as the passage that is "fulfilled." The procedure borders on allegorizing in such a way as to be either philosophical or mythical or otherwise, but the fact that at the "fulfillment" terminus there is a historical event (real or supposed does not alter the interpretation) keeps this method from being purely speculative and fanciful.[7]

Another more important way that the early writers saw that the Scripture was fulfilled was in the fulfilling of the underlying meaning of a passage. This is especially illustrated in Jesus' teaching in the Sermon on the Mount where he emphasized the deeper meaning of the Scripture (cf. 5:17–48). This motif is seen also in certain sayings and accounts where the *inner* meaning of the Old Testament text is directly applied to the historical situation. For example, the text of Matthew 1:18–25 involves a quotation from Isaiah 7:14. Unfortunately the *inner* meaning of the original passage and the meaning indicated in Matthew's gospel is obscured by the usual debate over the "virgin." That Matthew (and Luke also) believed in a virgin birth is clear, but the passage does not emphasize that motif. The original passage was designed to demonstrate to Ahaz, the king, and to the people that Yahweh was going to deliver the people from the Syro-Ephraimitic alliance; and this deliverance was to be declared by the naming of the child, Immanuel, meaning "God is with us." Matthew used the passage to indicate that with the birth of this child God was indeed with the people once again, and this time for an even greater deliverance than Isaiah spoke about. For Isaiah spoke of God's deliverance from military conquest; Matthew spoke of God's deliverance from *the* major enemy of humankind, namely sin! This was to take place in and through the Person of Jesus of Nazareth, who was to Matthew, "God with us."

In Matthew's gospel Jesus was no longer simply a servant. That he was to suffer and that he must die were almost assumed, but the important aspect of this Gospel consisted in interpreting Jesus as a kingly figure, worthy of adoration. At his birth rich, powerful wise men came *to worship.* There is scarcely any secrecy motif remaining in Matthew. Almost all of the injunctions to secrecy which were found in Mark have been either omitted or changed in Matthew's account. This is especially pointed in the Matthean version of the reason for speaking in parables. In Mark the parabolic method was for the express purpose of obscuring the message so that people would not understand (cf. Mark 4:10–12). In Matthew's version parable was used so that people *would clearly see* and have no excuse when they rejected the message and the bringer of that message (cf. Matt. 13: 13–15).

A further note should perhaps be inserted here about how one interprets a parable. A parable is basically a story or event drawn from everyday life which makes a comparison.[8] The parable makes usually a single point and most of the surrounding details are simply "filler" to make the story more graphic. For example, there is no need to wrestle with or argue over what one should do with the "ethics" of the parable of the Treasure in the Field (cf. Matt. 13:44). The meaning is clear—the Kingdom is worth all that one has and every effort should be made to obtain it.

One further facet could be added in relation to understanding Jesus' teaching. Like most Oriental teaching, there is much of it that is done by *hyperbole,* exaggeration to make a point. It should be obvious that the injunction to "cut off one's hand if it offends you" should be taken in this vein, as should certain other of Jesus' teachings (cf. Matt. 19:24; Mark 9:43–48).

These teaching methods illustrate the fact, often overlooked, that Jesus taught as a wise man in much the same manner as those who disseminated the practical proverbs of the Old Testament. Many of his sayings fall into this type of literary category and one must be careful not to construct absolute ethical doctrines from practical rules for everyday living. For example, the teachings in the Sermon on the Mount about getting along with one's neighbor are good illustrations (cf. Matt. 5:38–42). These verses have given rise to all sorts of interpretations, but they basically are practical rules for everyday living and it is not legitimate to build theological doctrines from them.

The Jesus of Matthew's Gospel is a King-Messiah, to be recognized by all who will, and he is the fulfillment of the true Judaism and the teacher of the new people of God.

Luke

The Gospel of Luke is the first part of a two-part story, the conclusion coming in Acts. This literary work depicts the origin and spread of the Christian movement. The Gospel portrait of Jesus by Luke is much loved. Whereas in Mark Jesus is a man of action opposing the forces of Satan, and in Matthew a kingly teacher, in the Gospel of Luke he is in many ways the man for all people! One of the chief emphases of Luke's two-volume work is that this Jesus is Messiah not of the Jews only but of the entire world. He is the friend and champion of the poor and the outcast (and women would be included in this category). In Matthew his birth is greeted by rich wise men, but in Luke it is announced to the ordinary shepherds doing their daily duties in the field.

Luke emphasizes true piety, piety meaning the awareness of and the dependence upon God's presence in life and in the affairs of the world. The heroes in Luke are truly "pious" people (cf. 1:5f.; 1:26f.; 2:25f., etc.). Closely connected with this motif is Luke's emphasis on the Holy Spirit and the place of the Spirit in the lives of people. This theme is more prominent in Acts but also has a real place in Luke's Gospel.

Perhaps the most important theme is that of Luke's insistence on the universality of the Christian "good news." This Jesus was not simply a Jewish Messiah; he was a savior for the world. In Mark and Matthew Jesus begins his ministry by preaching or teaching about the Kingdom of God, but in Luke he begins by proclaiming in the Synagogue that the Scripture (Isaiah 61:1–2) was being fulfilled—that

Gentiles were to be included in God's Kingdom! (cf. Luke 4:16–30).

Closely related is the emphasis in Luke upon the Christian movement as one that in no way challenged or was a threat to the political *status quo*. Christians were not subversive traitors who were scheming and plotting to overthrow the Emperor and the Empire. They were good law-abiding citizens who were in reality good for the Roman government, and the charges brought against them were always the result of human jealousy or misunderstanding and religious opposition from the Jews or pagans which had nothing to do with the violation of Roman law.

The Jesus of Luke's Gospel cared for the poor, the outcast, women, sometimes even the rich! Individuals are perhaps more important here than anywhere else in the New Testament. In the collection of parables in chapter 15, the emphasis is upon the one lost sheep, the one lost coin, the *two* lost sons. If religion has to do with daily life, this Gospel portrays a truly religious Messiah.

An Overview of the Synoptic Portrait of Jesus

No attempt has been made to examine the outlines of the three Synoptic Gospels, nor has there been an examination in any detail of the life and ministry of Jesus as portrayed there. This is because of the fact that in spite of the religious differences in emphasis, there remains among the three Gospels a fairly consistent picture of Jesus and his teaching.

It does not need to be repeated that the Gospels do not intend to give a biography of Jesus according to modern historical methodology. They were not intended to be biographical in that sense. What they do attempt to do is to portray Jesus as the people understood him from both the traditions about him and their own experience of what he and his teaching had meant to them and the significance of all that he was and continued to be.

Chronologically speaking, the Synoptics depict a ministry for Jesus of from six to no more than eighteen months, centering chiefly in Galilee with one trip to Jerusalem which culminated in his death. According to the Synoptic account, Jesus ate the Passover meal with his disciples on Thursday evening (the Jewish day is counted from sundown to sundown, approximately 6 P.M. to 6 P.M.), was later arrested, tried, taken to Pilate (in Luke he is also tried before Herod who could find no wrong in him), finally found guilty (probably a charge of political subversion or agitation against Rome), condemned to die, crucified, and buried. All this took place before the beginning of the Sabbath (Friday at 6 P.M.). His followers were scattered and disillusioned. It appeared that this movement had ceased to exist.

But, the Gospels all are in agreement that by Sunday morning Jesus was gone from the tomb. The accounts differ somewhat but they are certain of several points. Jesus' body is gone from the tomb. Jesus appeared to some of them and continued to do so for some time. Jesus' resurrection is unique, but none of them claims to understand how it happened or even *exactly* what happened. They are one in stating, nevertheless, that it was the resurrection that turned this frightened and disorganized band of bewildered followers into a dynamic group which took its message to the people of that time. The resurrection alone, however, was not regarded as *the* proof. It was seen, rather, as only the *final* proof, for these people proclaimed not simply a Risen Lord but a Person who had lived among them. What was he like? What did he teach? What did he do? All these aspects entered into the total picture of the Person the early Church proclaimed to be the Messiah of God who had come to bring a new relationship with God to humanity. Jesus came to bridge the gap between God and the human race and to do for humanity what it could not do for itself, i.e., restore the broken relationship between God and humanity by an action that dealt with man's sin. The impact of his ministry and the meaning of his resurrection is perhaps best summarized in Matthew's account of the birth narrative: ". . . and you will call his name Jesus [Hebrew, Joshua], for he will save his people from their sins" (1:21). How reminiscent of the new covenant passage in Jeremiah 31:31–34!

Apart from the impact of his personality and life which convinced those closest to him that he was uniquely the Son of God, there was also the impact of his teaching. The central theme in the Synoptic Gospels was the idea of the Kingdom of God. To say that this concept has been greatly debated would be a gross understatement![9] What exactly did Jesus mean by the term? Some argue that it is an entirely "this-worldly" concept to be realized within the historical process by either evolutionary or revolutionary means. Others feel that it has to be an entirely "other-worldly" concept. Some argue that it is a "realized" entity already present in this moment, while others argue that it is totally in the future.

These diverse elements in the teaching of Jesus as it is contained in the Gospels on this issue lead to the conclusion that the "Kingdom of God" is not a single, self-contained, easily definable, delineated structure but rather a combination of various ideas which are not presented in the Gospel traditions in a systematic way. This may be the result of the manner and mode in which the tradition was utilized, the lack of complete clarity about the teaching on the part of the disciples, or it may even reflect a non-systematic approach to the subject by Jesus himself. There do seem to be, however, several features and characteristics that are clear and are witnessed to in each of the levels of tradition.

Primarily the emphasis is upon the idea that the Kingdom is *God's* kingdom. It is not a human institution which can be made or developed by humanity. It is totally a gift of God, but people are summoned to work in the Kingdom and to commit their lives to it. This is exceedingly reminiscent of the call to Abraham; it is quite like the old covenant and doctrine of election! Further, this Kingdom is the means by which the Kingdom of Satan, that powerful force which has enslaved the human race and added to the miseries of human existence, would be defeated and destroyed.

The summons of Jesus' teaching to accept the Kingdom is based upon his conviction that the Kingdom was to be a *transforming power* in the lives of people. This Kingdom is centered in God; it is not some earthly Utopia nor some apocalyptic disaster which would put an end to human history as it has been known. There are some elements in the teaching that could be interpreted in these ways, but at the heart of the issue is the belief that God had entered into the world of human affairs in such a way and to a degree not previously known. Jesus conceived of this Kingdom as a growing dynamic entity, not static or stagnant. The only limitation to the greatness of the Kingdom, the sovereign reign of God, appears to be the failure of human beings to commit themselves to it and to labor in it.

God's Kingdom, then, is his activity to redeem mankind and to establish his sovereignty over the entire human race. Through this activity his sovereignty is established beyond all doubt and his reign recognized as eternal.

A closely related and also much debated theme is that of the eschatology of the Kingdom. In this point also many different interpretations have been espoused. The extremes are perhaps easiest to formulate. There are those who believe that Jesus' teaching about the Kingdom was basically that of a literal apocalyptic scheme. The Kingdom would come in the future when God dramatically and directly intervened in the historical process. Jesus believed that this would happen soon and that he would in some way play a direct part in the event. And there are teachings contained in the Synoptics that can be used for supporting such a conclusion (cf. Matthew 24–25; Mark 13; Luke 17, 21).

At the other end of the spectrum are those who believe that Jesus thought of the Kingdom as a present possession, a present reality. This is generally called "realized" eschatology. Those scholars who advocate this interpretation believe that Jesus used apocalyptic terminology, but really reinterpreted the apocalyptic content. But the disciples and the early Church, so thoroughly saturated with the apocalyptic thinking of the time, gave apocalyptic meaning and content to sayings of Jesus which were not originally intended to be taken apocalyptically. And there are some teachings of Jesus that can be easily understood as viewing the Kingdom as already present (cf. certain parables in Mark 4 and parallels; Matt. 2:28; Luke 11:20; 17:20–21; etc.).

But most scholars feel that the truth lies somewhere in between. That there was a sense in which the Kingdom had come and was realized in the ministry of Jesus is not debatable; but neither is the view that Jesus himself looked for the consummation of the Kingdom in the future. The Kingdom is "now and not yet," "here, but yet to come." And the clear answer to this problem comes from the teaching of Jesus that the time of the consummation of the Kingdom is not the major concern of his people; it is the concern of all persons to accept the commitment to enter the Kingdom and to work in that commitment. All else is irrelevant!

Living in the Kingdom, i.e., participating in this new life, brings certain obligations. Many speak about the "ethics of the Kingdom," but there is no set of external rules or regulations which characterize Jesus' teaching at this point. The command is simple yet difficult: ". . . You shall love the Lord your God with all your heart, and with all your soul, and with all your mind, and with all your strength . . . [and] you shall love your neighbor as yourself" (Mark 12:29–31). Jesus therefore made the Kingdom ethic a "relational" matter, not a propositional one. And in such a structure it is not the "letter of the law" that is important so much as the attitude and motivation which are exhibited. One is reminded again of Jesus' famous "antitheses" teachings in Matthew 5:17f.

There is one further issue which needs to be discussed. That concerns the "titles" which are given to Jesus in the Synoptic Gospels. It has already been indicated that one is "Son of God"; each of the writers in his own way believed that Jesus was God's son in a unique sense. This was emphasized by Jesus' own use of the term, *"Abba,"* which is the Aramaic equivalent of "Daddy." To speak of God in such a casual and intimate way was unthinkable at this time when God was far removed from humankind. Therefore there was a unique and special relationship that existed between Jesus and God which the Gospel writers designate by "Son of God."

Another is the title "Messiah." Some scholars are quick to point out that Jesus never used this term of himself, and therefore he did not consider himself to be the Messiah. Whether this is true or not, the Gospel writers understood him to be the Messiah, depicted his ministry as a Messianic ministry, and in each account made the central turning point of the Gospel the confession of Peter that he was indeed the Messiah (cf. Mark 8:27f.; Matt. 16:13f.; Luke 9:18f.). This recognition by the disciples was understood by the three Gospel writers to be a great moment in Jesus' ministry. From this point on the emphasis in his teaching changed; his relation to his disciples and the direction of his ministry were re-oriented in such a way that the emphasis was more upon the smaller group preparing them for his impending death, and the teaching about the necessity for and meaning of that death.

There is one other title found almost exclusively in the Gospels which has caused scholars much concern over the years. This is the term, "Son of Man." There are several possibilities as to the meaning of this term. In the Semitic background, out of which it came, the term can mean simply "man." This was a common expression. There are those who argue that the term also could be used as a circumlocution for "I", but this seems to be rather remote. It could also be a title, for it seems to have been used as such in Daniel 7 and in the apocalyptic work designated 1 Enoch (cf. chs. 46; 62; 69). In Daniel the Son of Man is a designation for the "people of the most high," a collective term, whereas in 1 Enoch the figure appears to be a type of "heavenly" being who exercises some of the functions of a Messianic figure.

Exactly how the term is used in the Synoptics is a matter of debate. It is true that there seems to be three basic types of "Son of Man" sayings.[10] First there was a group of sayings in which the Son of Man is viewed as an "earthly" person; a second group which connected the "Son of Man" and suffering; and a third group in which the "Son of Man" was a figure who would appear in the future. Scholars interpret these three catagories in various and sundry ways! Some accept all, some reject all, and some pick and choose among the catagories! There are those who feel that Jesus was *not* speaking of himself when he used the term but of someone who would come in the future. Others feel that this was a title given to Jesus by the early Church.

It does not fit the purpose here to attempt to unravel the mysteries of this term, but one thing is clear from our perspective. The Gospel writers, all, believed that Jesus used this term and used it of himself. It was really the only self-designation that we have which was attributed to Jesus himself! It was used nowhere else of him (except in Stephen's speech in Acts 7 and in the vision in Revelation 1) and is found in the Synoptics only on the lips of Jesus.[11] And it appears to be used in the Gospels as the designation of Jesus as suffering-messiah.

Miracles

It may be wise before departing from the Synoptics to discuss briefly the miracles in the Gospels. Contrary to much popular thinking, Jesus was not unique in being able to perform "wonders." Nor did the disciples or others believe in him as Messiah, Son of God, because of these actions. What were called miracles to a different time and culture may or may not be miracles to us. But that is to miss the point.

The miracles were in the Synoptic Gospels *signs*—signs pointing not to the nature of Jesus but to the fact that the Kingdom of God was present. These marvelous happenings were indications that *God* was acting on behalf of his people. As already indicated, Jesus was not the only person who was able to do these things. When accused of casting out demons in the name of Satan, Jesus asked, "By whom do your sons cast them out?" (Luke 11:19).

The types of miracles Jesus performed were: (1) exorcisms, the most numerous; (2) physical healings; (3) raising people from the dead; (4) nature miracles. All of these have to do with the power of God's Kingdom over the realm of Satan. They were utilized in much the same way in the Synoptics as the miracles of Elijah in demonstrating the superiority of Yahweh over Baal. Cf. chapter 4, pp. 50–51.

Jesus' performance of miracles also had some differences from the miracle workers of his day. The miracle was not done to exalt the miracle worker, but to point to something else, namely, the presence of the Kingdom of God. There were no magical charms or incantations or the like involved in the miracles of Jesus. And most importantly Jesus' miracles required faith—i.e., trust. This faith did not always have to be the faith of the person upon whom the miracle was performed, but could be the faith of those around (cf. Mark 2:1–11 and parallels; Mark 9:14f. and parallels). In fact, the reader was plainly told that where there was no faith, there were no miracles (cf. Mark 6:5–6)!

Again the biblical emphasis upon the event plus the interpretation of the event as being revelation is demonstrated, not only in the interpretation of the miracles but in the entire ministry of Jesus!

The most stupendous miracle of the Gospel accounts is, of course, Jesus' resurrection. Many attempts have been made through the years to explain what really happened here. Jesus' disciples stole his body and hid it; Jesus was not really dead but had only fainted into a deep sleep; the disciples wanted to see Jesus again so much that they hallucinated an image of Him. There are various other explanations in addition, but according to the New Testament witness something remarkable happened to transform this frightened and disorganized band of men into a group that was ready to die for what they knew they had experienced. In other words, these resurrection stories are the result of something that happened (exactly what even the New Testament writers are not quite sure) to create faith in the disciples. It is really *not* logical to think that their faith produced the resurrection stories, for the disciples did not fully understand before and were still confused even after the resurrection appearances!

There are a number of persons who are somewhat confused about the nature of the resurrection. However one of the clearest explanations, religiously speaking, is found in the following excerpts from G. E. Ladd's *A Theology of the New Testament.* "Bultmann says that the resuscitation of a corpse is incredible. Even if this should be a valid objection, it carries no weight, for the New Testament does not picture the resurrection of Jesus in terms of the resuscitation of a corpse, but as *the emergence within time and space of a new order of life.* . . . Jesus' resurrection is not the restoration to physical life of a dead body; it is the emergence of a new order of life. It is the embodiment in time and space of eternal life."[12]

Additional Readings

Bible: Mark; Matthew; Luke

Secondary Material:

Kee, H. C. *Jesus in History: An Approach to the Study of the Gospels.* New York: Harcourt, Brace & World, 1970.

Beare, F. W. *The Earliest Records of Jesus.* New York: Abingdon Press, 1962.

Briggs, R. C. *Interpreting the New Testament Today.* New York: Abingdon Press, 1973, pp. 18–137.

Saunders, Ernest W. *Jesus in the Gospels.* Englewood Cliffs, New Jersey: Prentice-Hall, Inc., 1967.

Jeremias, Joachim. *Rediscovering the Parables.* New York: Charles Scribner's Sons, 1966.

Anderson, Hugh, ed. *Jesus.* Englewood Cliffs, New Jersey: Prentice-Hall, Inc., 1967.

Ladd, G. E. *I Believe in the Resurrection of Jesus.* Grand Rapids, Mich.: Wm. B. Eerdmans Publishing Co., 1975.

Notes Chapter 7

1. These traditions were later written down as the *Mishnah.* A later collection of interpretations of the Mishnah was called the *Gemara.* Together these form the great "learning" of the Jewish people relating to the Torah called the *Talmud.*

2. In 66 A.D. war broke out between the Jewish people in Palestine and Rome. This attempt at freedom was quashed rather severely in 70 A.D. with the capture of Jerusalem and the destruction of the Temple by the Roman general Titus, who later became emperor.

3. These may be the ancient equivalent of the switch-blade set!

4. The two basic "forms" are the pronouncement-story (a story focusing on a saying of Jesus) and the miracle story. The first follows a basic pattern: (1) The setting is described; (2) there is some action which causes some response on the part of Jesus; (3) the pronouncement by Jesus; (4) the reaction of the bystanders. The miracle story follows its pattern as well: (1) A need is described; (2) Jesus acts in such a way as to effect a "cure"; (3) the response of the bystanders. For illustrations cf. Mark 2:23–28; 3:1–6, etc.

5. This problem was brought to the attention of New Testament scholarship in 1901 by Wilhelm Wrede, *The Messianic Secret in The Gospels,* trans. J.C.G. Greig (Cambridge: J. Clark, 1971).

6. It was this feature of Mark's account which led to the downfall of the idea of the "priority of Mark," i.e., Mark as a basic historical, non-theological account of Jesus' life, and to the understanding that Mark was indeed a highly theological document. Cf. again Wrede.

7. Cf. other examples in Matthew 1:22–25; 2:17–18; etc.

8. One must be careful not to confuse parable and allegory. An allegory is a story in which there is a hidden meaning under every detail in the narrative. There are a few allegories in the Gospels, but these are usually already interpreted (cf. Matthew 13:36f.; otherwise the stories should be interpreted as parables).

9. For a rather full discussion of the interpretations cf. Göstra Lundström, *The Kingdom of God in the Teaching of Jesus,* trans. Joan Bulman (Richmond: John Knox Press, 1963); also Norman Perrin, *The Kingdom of God in the Teaching of Jesus,* The New Testament Library Series (Philadelphia: The Westminster Press, 1963).

10. For a classic statement on the "Son of Man" sayings, cf. Rudolf Bultmann, *The Theology of the New Testament,* trans. K. Grobel (New York: Charles Scribner's Sons, 1951), Vol. I, p. 30f.

11. Is it not odd (if this were a title given to him by the early Church) that this term is nowhere else used of Jesus? It would appear logical to assume that this was Jesus' own "title." Whether it was misunderstood by the disciples and the early Church is another matter.

12. G.E. Ladd, *A Theology of the New Testament* (Grand Rapids, Michigan: Wm. B. Eerdman's Publishing Co., 1974), pp. 323–24. Used by permission.

8
*The Early Church
and the Career of Paul*

There is no question but that the resurrection of Jesus was *the* event which gave rise to the development of the early Church. Even though the Gospels do not agree in their accounts as to all the specific details, they are at one in affirming that God had done a marvelous, even stupendous, thing. While the resurrection is not a historically provable event, something happened of such a magnitude to turn the frustrated and frightened band of disciples into a group of persons who were committed and fearless in their proclamation of all that God had done in and through Jesus, even to the point of martyrdom for their convictions.

Since the book of Acts is the basic source for information about the history of the early Church, it must be remembered that Acts is the second volume of the two volume work which began with the Gospel of Luke. And the same emphases of the Gospel of Luke continue in this sequel (cf. pp. 98–99).

The account begins with the Ascension scene which occurred forty days after the resurrection.[1] At the time of this last appearance to them, Jesus instructed the disciples to wait in Jerusalem for the gift of the Spirit, and then said: ". . . you shall be my witnesses in Jerusalem and in all Judea and Samaria and to the end of the earth" (Acts 1:8b). These words form the basis for the outline and progress of the Church's development as outlined in the book of Acts.

Before turning directly to the development of the early Church, it would assist in understanding to be aware of some of the basic beliefs of the early Christians. Already discussed has been the importance of the belief in the resurrection of Jesus, but there were other important aspects as well. These are included in what many New Testament scholars call the *kerygma* or "proclamation" of the early Church.[2] There are basically six points which constantly recur in the New Testament witnesses:

(1) The New Age promised in the Scripture has now dawned.

(2) This has come about through the Life-Death-Resurrection of Jesus of Nazareth who was a descendent of David. It was emphasized that Jesus lived a life characterized by good works, was unjustly condemned and crucified, but was raised from the dead by the power of God.

(3) Because of the resurrection Jesus has been exalted to the right hand of God as head of the New Israel. One of the earliest confessions was "Jesus is Lord!" The term "Lord" probably has its background in the Old Testament concept of Yahweh who is referred to as "Lord." In other words, this confession is one which very closely identified God and Jesus and is one of the foundation stones for the later developed doctrine about Jesus called Christology.

(4) The Holy Spirit active in the Church is the sign that Jesus is still alive and present with those who believe in him.

(5) Jesus will return *soon* to consummate the Kingdom. This belief was a popular and strongly held conviction in the early Church. It is an apocalyptic motif which was literally interpreted by the Church. Whether this teaching actually went back to Jesus or was misunderstood by the disciples is not known for sure. Whatever the reason, however, this concept continued to persist even down to the writing of the last book in the New Testament canon. The technical term for the return of Jesus is *Parousia.*

(6) The *kerygma* concludes with an appeal to the hearers to repent and accept the new life which was being offered to them.

These are the elements of the early preaching, and it could be legitimately argued that the entire New Testament is a commentary on these points. It should be noted at this juncture that the early Church did not at first think of itself as a separate entity from Judaism. These early believers worshiped in the Temple and in the Synagogue. They also met in private homes. Their basic cultic practices were the rites of baptism and the Eucharist (thanksgiving meal). At first the Eucharist was probably a full scale meal (called the *agape,* or love feast), but because of certain abuses it became a smaller ritual service somewhere along the line. (The same fate awaited the injunction to greet each other with a holy kiss!) The important point to remember is that these persons believed there was no break between the old Israel and the new, that there was no difference in the elective purpose of God for the new Israel vis-à-vis the old Israel, that there was one God and therefore one redemptive purpose and process.

The critical issue in the kerygmatic proclamation was the "event" of Jesus. Some argue that the simple religion which Jesus espoused was "perverted" into a highly speculative theological system about Jesus. It is true that the one who proclaimed the centrality of the Kingdom of God had become the one who was proclaimed! Whether this development was legitimate is a matter of interpretation, but those who knew this person "in the flesh" and experienced the power of the resurrection did not feel that it was illegitimate to make the switch—in fact, they probably did so without any thought about inconsistency at all. The impact of this total experience transformed the disciples into proclaimers of the new life available to all in Jesus.

As the Church spread into the Gentile world, the term *Messiah* (Greek, *Christos*) became the distinguishing word for these people. It was probably at first a term of derision, "the Messiah people," but as with many such "put downs" it was worn with pride and later became *the* name for the followers of Jesus. It was not until the Church had spread, however, that the followers of the Christ were first called "Christians"; this was at Antioch in Syria (cf. Acts 11:26). Up until that time they were variously called "Galileans" (cf. Acts 1:11; 2:7; 13:31), "disciples" (cf. Acts 2:44), the "Way" (cf. Acts 9:2), even "Nazarenes" (Acts 24:5; perhaps cf. also Matt. 2:23).

In the beginning of the development of the early Church there was very little organizational structure. The "Twelve" held, naturally, the place of authority. Even the number was viewed as special, so much so that a person was chosen by lot to take the place of Judas; but after he was chosen, nothing more was heard about him (cf. Acts 1:21–26)! There was also early on an attempt at economic communal living which ultimately proved to be disastrous (cf. Acts 4:32–37), because the people in the Church had made no provision for the future. In fact, they did not feel that it was necessary to do so since the Parousia was indeed right around the corner. The selling of property and the subsequent gift of that money to the Church's common fund was not mandatory, however, and the story of Ananias and Sapphira should not be interpreted in that manner (cf. Acts 5:1–11). Their sin was the sin of hypocrisy, which, next to the rejection of Jesus as Messiah and Lord, was probably the sin *par excellance* in the life of the early Church. It was their conviction that it was the hypocrisy of the Jewish religious leaders which had led to the rejection and crucifixion of Jesus.[3]

As with any growing body, the Church experienced problems which necessitated some organization and structure. The first account of this came when the Greek-speaking Christians in Jerusalem claimed that their widows were being neglected in the "daily distribution" (Acts 6:1–6). To solve this problem the Church appointed seven men to perform these types of duties, thus allowing the apostles to continue their basic ministry of preaching.

The growing Church in Jerusalem encountered opposition almost from the very beginning with the arrest of Peter and John (Acts 4) and others (Acts 5:18f.). This opposition finally erupted into a mob scene when Stephen, one of the seven, delivered a fiery speech indicting the Jewish people for their sins which incited the crowd into a stoning episode. This triggered a persecution of the Christians with the result that many were scattered throughout the area of Judea and Samaria (Acts 8:1).

The emphasis of Luke on the universality of the gospel, that the Christian life was for all people, began to take center stage at this point in the Acts narrative. This section (chapters 8–12) described the Church as expanding, and at this juncture Saul was called into the ministry to the Gentiles (Acts 9); Peter learned that all people are important to God and that the Church must open its doors to the Gentiles (Acts 10); and more persecution followed with the martyrdom of James (the brother of John) at the hands of Herod Agrippa I and the imprisonment of Peter. Herod died under peculiar circumstances, and the Christians naturally interpreted that as the judgment of God (Acts 12).

By this stage of Acts the Church was established in Jerusalem, in spite of the persecution, and in the area generally known as Palestine. Its chief center had moved, however, to Antioch in Syria, but in all probability it had begun to spread to other places as well.

The Hellenistic World

Before turning to the career of Paul, the world to which Paul preached his gospel should be examined briefly. It has often been assumed that the Graeco-Roman world no longer believed in the old gods, i.e., Zeus, Jupiter, and the rest, and that there was in fact a huge religious vacuum waiting to be filled at the proper moment by the message of the Christian Church. Visions of a great, overpowering, unnumbered mass of persons turning almost immediately to embrace the new religion have been imagined. Such a notion could hardly be farther from the truth!

To be sure, there was a decline in the worship of the old gods, but even so many people still believed in them.[4] Otherwise, however, there were probably more religions and religious philosophies actively being espoused and pursued in this time than almost at any other period in the history of humanity. People still worshiped the old gods; countless gods of the mystery religions were very popular in this period; local gods and goddesses, and religious-type philosophies such as Stoicism, Epicureanism, and that of the Cynics flourished. In addition to these more well defined groups there was also a prevailing quasi-religious thought pattern which permeated much of the thinking of the time. The ideas prevalent in this pattern have come to be known as *Gnosticism. Gnosis* was the Greek word for knowledge, and thus the basic characteristic of this ideology was salvation by knowledge.

Even though the Gnostic thought patterns were not "finalized" into specific religious systems until much later, nevertheless many Gnostic ideas were prevalent in various types of religious groups in much the same way that apocalyptic permeated many of the Jewish groups in Palestine at the time of Jesus. The basic motif of this pattern was that there is a radical dualism between spirit and matter, God and the created world. It was held that God was transcendent above the created order and did not create, nor does he govern, the universe. The created world was made by lesser beings or powers which exercise dominion over the earth and all on it. The "spirit" of human beings could be traced to some divine spark that somehow managed to permeate this created order, but that spirit is imprisoned in the material "flesh" of this world. It is asleep waiting to be awakened by knowledge. This knowledge consists in essence of the makeup of the structure of the "over-world," the connecting maze between the world we know and the world of spirit (sometimes called the *pleroma* or "fulness"). When the knowledge of this structure is "revealed" to a person, it enabled the spirit at death to make its way through the maze of the structure of the over-world and thus be freed into the realm of light, spirit, God.

Each Gnostic system had a myth of its own in which these details were concretized and personified. In some, perhaps most, of the systems a transcendent savior was involved who intervened in cosmic history, and to whom the devotees were indebted for his making available this knowledge in order for them to escape the vicious cycle which enslaves them.[5] As indicated, this type of thinking was quite prevalent in the first century, especially among the Greeks and Romans.

Paul

The great Apostle Paul was not a stranger to the Hellenistic world. According to tradition he had been reared in the town of Tarsus in Asia Minor, a site of "university learning." According to Acts he was a Roman citizen, but exactly how he came to be such is not known. He supposedly studied at the feet of Gamaliel, one of the most famous of all the rabbis, and was in Jerusalem at the time of the stoning of Stephen. According to tradition (and from certain remarks in his letters), he was not an attractive person, physically speaking. Before his experience on the Damascus Road, his great zeal for the Law had led him to be a persecutor of those who he felt were perverting the great faith of Abraham and Moses and the prophets. He even had received special authority to locate and bring back to Jerusalem those who were followers of the "Way" (cf. Acts 9:1–2).

After his "conversion" or "call" experience on the road to Damascus, he was brought to a certain Ananias in Damascus and remained until a plot against his life necessitated his escape over the walls in a basket by night (cf. Acts 9:10–25)! The disciples at Jerusalem were afraid of him; and when another plot was devised against him, he was sent off to Tarsus. According to his letter to the Galatians Paul said that he went to Arabia before going to Jerusalem. Whatever the chronology, which is impossible to follow precisely, Paul returned to Tarsus and remained there for some time. He then was "remembered" by Barnabas, a leader of the Church in Antioch, and Paul was brought by Barnabas to serve in the Church there (Acts 11:19–26).

After a visit with Barnabas to Jerusalem to deliver some assistance to the Church there because of a famine, Barnabas and Saul (his name had not yet been changed) were set apart to embark on an evangelizing journey. They along with some others sailed for Cyprus to begin the famous "missionary journeys." Barnabas was the leader on this first effort. In accordance with his usual emphases, Luke recorded the first convert on the first journey as none other than Sergius Paulus, the Roman proconsul, governor of Cyprus! What better way to emphasize that this new religious movement was not politically subversive. It was here that Saul's name was changed to Paul; and contrary to any popular opinion there was nothing esoteric about the change. *Paul* is probably the Greek equivalent of the Hebrew-Aramaic *Saul.*

After leaving Cyprus they came to Asia Minor (part of what is now Turkey) where John Mark left them to return home. Their itinerary then took them to Pisidian Antioch, to Iconium, to Lystra, and to Derbe, from which point they retraced their steps (except for Cyprus) and returned to Syrian Antioch. On this journey the basic patterns for the missionary activity were established and these same patterns seem to have been followed throughout the journeys. They first preached in the Synagogue (if there was one); they usually encountered bitter opposition from the Jews and/or from the Gentiles, but in spite of the problems, churches were established. Sometimes the opposition became highly dangerous, as in Lystra where Paul was stoned and left for dead (Acts 14:19f.).

Many of those who did accept the preaching of Paul were probably Gentiles known as "God-fearers." These were persons who were attracted to Judaism because of its ethical demands, high standards, and strict monotheism, but who refused to become full members of the Jewish community. These persons attended the Synagogue meetings and upheld the ethical requirements of the law but rejected the ceremonial. It is easy to see why the preaching of Paul appealed to them.

The success of the missionary work, however, led to a large problem in the Church. Should the new Gentile converts be required to keep the ceremonial aspects of the Jewish law? The debate connected with this problem (whenever it occurred) was placed by Luke at this juncture in his Acts account. The Jerusalem Council, depicted in Acts 15, was called for the purpose of resolving the question of what should Gentiles be required to do vis-à-vis the old ceremonial regulations. A serious meeting took place, but the exact "solution" is debated because of textual problems and the ambiguity of the text. The general meaning seems to be clear, however. The Gentiles were not bound to keep the ceremonial laws, except that they should be sensitive to the food laws when having table fellowship with former Jews. They further should abstain from any idolatry, naturally, and probably there was an injunction to high ethical conduct and character (cf. Acts 15:19–21, 28–29).[6]

In any event, Paul and Barnabas returned to Antioch and prepared to leave on another journey. Because John Mark had left them on the first journey, Paul did not want him to accompany them again. Barnabas insisted, however, which caused him and Paul to separate, Barnabas and Mark going to Cyprus (we hear of them no more) while Paul and Silas took the land route and returned to the Churches in Galatia established on the first journey. At Lystra Paul found young Timothy, the uncircumcised son of a Greek father and a Jewish mother, whom he decided to take with him. In order for Timothy to be of value to Paul, especially when he preached in the Synagogue, Timothy was circumcised, not for religious reasons but for purely practical ones. An uncircumcised person in the "inner" circle of the Synagogues would have been an unforgiveable affront to the Jews.

Paul then traveled to Troas where he was summoned to Macedonia. The first recorded convert on European soil is Lydia, a businesswoman (note Luke's emphasis on the importance of women), after which he cast out an "evil spirit" from a girl in Philippi. For this he and his companions were beaten and thrown into prison. Appealing to his Roman citizenship, Paul wrenched an apology from the leaders and went on to other locales. In almost every place trouble followed, in Thessalonica and Beroea especially. He then came to

Athens where he delivered the famous Areopagus (or Mars Hill) speech, which was not a kerygmatic proclamation (cf. Acts 17:16–34). The Athenians simply laughed at him, and even though a few did believe, there is no evidence of a strong, growing Church at Athens during this period.

Where he did have success, however, was strange indeed. Corinth was infamous for its immorality, both that which was "normal" for seaport towns and also that which was connected with the different religions of the city. Whatever the reason, Paul found a receptive audience here, established a rather strong (if not always "proper") Church, and remained for almost eighteen months. It was at Corinth that we have the only datable event in his life. Gallio, the Roman proconsul of Achaea, came to the office in 51 or 52 A.D. (this is known from an inscription). It was shortly after Gallio arrived that the Jews at Corinth accused Paul before Gallio of "persuading men to worship God contrary to the law" (Acts 18:13). Naturally, in Luke's account nothing was amiss as far as Gallio and the Roman law were concerned, and Paul was released (cf. Acts 18:12f.).

He left then for Ephesus, perhaps to prepare the way for his long stay there which would come shortly, and returned to Caesarea. There is some doubt as to whether he went to Jerusalem at this time, but he did come back again to Antioch in Syria. After a short while he left to return by the land route to the churches in Galatia, but went rather quickly to Ephesus where he remained for almost three years.

While in Ephesus there was a riot caused by the silversmith, Demetrius, who was upset because Paul's preaching had hurt his sales! This scene was a dangerous one (cf. Acts 19:23f.), and there were obviously other problems which Paul encountered in Ephesus which are not recorded in Acts (cf. 1 Cor. 15:32; 16:9; 2 Cor. 1:8–9). Whether Paul was actually imprisoned here is a debated point, and even though there is no explicit statement to that effect, there is every reason to believe that it is quite probable. In fact his life may very well have been in jeopardy (cf. Romans 16:3).

During his stay at Ephesus there were two basic problems apart from the local ones which occupied his time. Both concerned attempts on the part of some persons to discredit Paul and the gospel he preached. The first revolved around the argument most popularly called the "Judaizing" controversy. Persons were arguing that in order to be a Christian, a convert was required to keep the ceremonial requirements of the Torah, particularly circumcision. This problem was centered in the Churches in Galatia where the basic charge against Paul was that he was not an apostle and therefore not preaching an "authentic" Gospel message.

The second problem was with the Corinthian Church. Having just come to the Christian faith from a life of "moral ease" in Corinth, the members of the Church were having great difficulties in adjusting to the Christian ethic. Paul attempted to deal with their problems, but further trouble came when someone(s) questioned Paul's authority there and aroused the membership against him. He made a trip from Ephesus to Corinth, where he met with a most unpleasant situation which caused him to leave and write to them a "painful" letter in which he rather sternly rebuked them for their conduct in general and their treatment of him in particular. This letter brought the people around; Paul returned to Corinth and spent the winter of 56–57 A. D. with them before he left for Jerusalem with the money he had collected from the Gentile churches to help relieve the economic problems of the Church in Jerusalem.

When he arrived in Jerusalem, another riot broke out (cf. Acts 21:27f.). Paul was then taken into protective custody by the Romans. He defended himself before the Sanhedrin (Acts 23) by arguing that he was being tried simply because he believed in the resurrection. Since some of the tribunal were Pharisees, they saw nothing wrong with that.[7] But the dissention became so great even here that he had to be rescued by the Roman soldiers. When a plot against his life was later discovered, he was removed to Caesarea, the Roman seat of government, and kept there for almost two years. At the time of the change of the Roman governor (Felix to Festus), Paul was asked if he did not wish to be taken to Jerusalem for trial in the matter. Realizing that there was great danger in this course of action and fearing that Festus may send him anyway (to ingratiate himself with the Jews and their leaders), Paul appealed to Caesar, as was his right as a Roman citizen (Acts 25).

The voyage to Italy was made even though it was interrupted by a shipwreck (Acts 27:13f.). The party finally arrived at Rome where

Paul was greeted by some of the Christians there. He was placed under house arrest and met many people and preached freely. The book of Acts concludes with this statement: "And he lived there two full years at his own expense, and welcomed all who came to him, preaching the kingdom of God and teaching about the Lord Jesus Christ quite openly and unhindered" (Acts 28:30–31).

What was the outcome of the matter? Did he appear before Caesar? Was he released? These questions are not answered by Luke in Acts, and several theories have been presented to explain Luke's silence. Luke died before he could finish the work. He had planned a third volume which he was not able to write. He did not know what happened to Paul, i.e., his sources were incomplete. There could be truth in any of these theories, but most of them seem rather strained. Although the traditions about Paul in Rome were varied, one point is consistent. Paul (along with Peter) met a martyr's death in Rome at the time of the Neronic persecution ca. 64 A. D. Whether he realized his dream of going to Spain is not known. There is some evidence that he was able to go. Whatever happened, Luke probably knew that Paul and Peter had been martyred and therefore he ended his work before those events transpired. It would have been very embarrassing for Luke who had spent two full volumes writing about the political innocence of the Christian movement and its leaders to have to conclude his "documentary" by admitting that both the leader of the "Jewish" segment of the Christian Church and the leader of the Gentile segment of the Christian Church were martyred by a Roman persecution led by Nero. It would have destroyed a great deal of what he had been attempting to demonstrate throughout his two-volume work.

Additional Readings

Bible: Acts

Secondary Material:

Bruce, F. F. *New Testament History,* rev. ed. London: Oliphants, 1971, pp. 195–408.

Caird, G. B. *The Apostolic Age.* London: Gerald Duckworth & Co., Ltd., 1955.

Elliott-Binns, L. E. *Galilean Christianity.* London: SCM Press, Ltd., 1956.

Filson, F. V. *Three Crucial Decades.* Richmond: John Knox Press, 1963.

Ladd, G. E. *The Young Church.* Bible Guide Series. New York: Abingdon Press, 1964.

Notes Chapter 8

1. One is reminded that the number forty is the biblical number for a certain completed period of time (cf. Gen. 7:12; Num. 13:25; 14:33; Judges 3:11; Mark 1:13).

2. Cf. C.H. Dodd, *The Apostolic Preaching and Its Developments* (New York: Harper & Row, 1951).

3. This point is strongly emphasized in the Synoptic Gospels (cf. especially Matthew 23), and it is very easy to understand how this would lead to an emphasis against this type of behavior among the early Christians.

4. Cf. Pausanias's accounts of the world of the second century A.D. in Greece. *Pausanias's Description of Greece,* translated and commentary by J.G. Frazer (New York: Macmillan Co., 1898), 6 Vols.

5. For an excellent presentation of this phenomenon, cf. Hans Jonas, *The Gnostic Religion* (Boston: Beacon Press, 1958).

6. If Galatians 2:1f. is Paul's account of this Council, it was also decided that Paul's primary purpose was to proclaim the gospel to the Gentiles.

7. Paul did not explain, according to the Acts account, that it was because he was proclaiming a particular resurrection that he was on trial before them!

9
Paul's Letters and Beliefs

Even though he was by his own admission not a physically appealing person and had some kind(s) of physical ailment, the New Testament writings contain many of Paul's letters; in fact, approximately twenty-five per cent of the New Testament was written by Paul. And these are the earliest of the New Testament literature.

Throughout the history of the Christian Church, leaders have looked to Paul's writings for their theology. It was long thought that the Synoptic Gospels depicted Jesus' simple religion; Paul, however, made a theological system of it. It is true that theologians of the Church have for centuries looked to Paul. Whether this is legitimate is another question, for of all the New Testament writings Paul's letters are probably the most "occasional." By this is meant that these letters were written to particular situations with particular problems containing Paul's considered judgments about what should or should not be done. In short, there is no systematic theology in Paul's writings, not even Romans. Certain principles and guidelines about his theological mind-set can be drawn from his writings, but one must always remember that all of what Paul thought and believed will not be contained in occasional writings.

Even though it is not appropriate here to write a detailed introduction to each of Paul's letters, it is especially helpful to know something about his correspondence with the churches. It should be made clear that, critically speaking, scholars argue over the "authentic" Pauline letters. Some argue that as few as three or four letters can be with certainty ascribed to Paul, while others argue that all those letters claiming Pauline authorship and one which doesn't (i.e., Hebrews) should be accepted as genuinely Pauline. The truth as usual probably lies somewhere between these two extremes. For the purposes of this study, the following will be considered as from the hand of Paul: 1 and 2 Thessalonians, 1 and 2 Corinthians, Galatians and Romans, Philippians, Colossians, and Philemon. There is enough doubt about Ephesians to justify omitting that book at this point, and it is almost universally agreed that Paul did not write the Pastoral Epistles (1 and 2 Timothy and Titus), even though fragments of genuine Pauline correspondence may be detected within these compositions. And Hebrews does not even claim to be by Paul at all; it was only later that it was attributed to him.

Paul's letters usually follow the same pattern as other letters of this period. The writing begins with a salutation followed by a thanksgiving. The body of the letter contains the basic discussion of the problems at hand. Many find that the body of Paul's letters can be divided into two sections—one more "theoretical" in that it addresses the problems and finds certain principles upon which to base the solutions; and secondly a section that is rather specific in terms of Christian living. Some say that the divisions are (1) "theological" and (2) "ethical." These terms may be useful, but in Paul's thinking there is no division between theology and ethics. And it may be doubtful if he were even aware that he did, in fact, usually follow that kind of pattern. After the body of the letter there would be some concluding remarks followed by a greeting written in Paul's own hand.[1]

As one reads Paul's letters, there are times when his thought is difficult to follow; it seems that he has introduced a thought but has digressed and then does not return to the original discussion. This is at least in part the result of the fact that Paul dictated his letters. Whether the same person transcribed each letter or whether there were different amanuenses is not known. If the latter, this would tend to explain some minor differences of style between certain letters which cause scholars some concern. Whatever the answer, Paul's mind was quick, active, and learned. Being also capable of being moved with emotion, he could argue logically, skip from point to point, change the meanings of words, or simply forget to finish a point. The content of his writings deserves and needs very careful attention.

It is advisable at this point to discuss briefly the background of the Pauline letters. This information will be extremely helpful in attempting to understand some of Paul's thinking on various issues.

The first of Paul's letters were those written to the Thessalonian Church. Which of the two epistles was written first is a debatable point, but it is enough to say that both were written in 49–50 A. D., probably from Corinth (perhaps one from Athens?). The letter known as 1 Thessalonians sees Paul relieved that the people have withstood persecution and have kept the faith. He attempted to answer questions for them (cf. 4:9–5:22) on the relationship between Christians within the Church, the problem of whether those who have died will miss participation in the Parousia, and exactly when the Parousia would occur.

Second Thessalonians is similar in many respects, but in this epistle Paul was admonishing the people to keep the faith in the face of persecution which was then going on. He attempted to clarify their thinking about the Parousia and the events that would precede it (ch. 2). His basic eschatological pattern here is that of an apocalyptic scheme literally interpreted. He admonished the people to stay busy, for it appears that some had quit their jobs to await the Parousia which would, they thought, occur very soon.

As is obvious these two short letters date from Paul's second journey. The remainder of his letters come from the third journey, primarily during his stay at Ephesus and from his imprisonment at Rome. The following date from the third journey and probably all except part of 2 Corinthians (written from Macedonia) and Romans (written from Corinth) originated in Ephesus between 54–56 A. D.: 1 Corinthians, 2 Corinthians, Galatians, Philippians.

It was a stormy time for Paul with the Corinthian Church, so much so that he wrote a minimum of four letters and made at least two visits! In 1 Corinthians 5:9 he had already written a letter to them to warn them against immoral people. This letter is lost unless 2 Corinthians 6:14–7:1 is a fragment of it as some scholars think. The second letter is 1 Corinthians which deals with one problem after another in the Church, some of which they wrote to him about (cf. 1 Cor. 7:1) and some of which (the "juiciest") came by word of mouth from "Chloe's people" (cf. 1 Cor. 1:11). The problems ranged from petty jealousy to gross immorality to theological inquiry about the resurrection. Paul attempted to answer each problem as best he could in the light of the traditions he had about Jesus and his teaching and Paul's own understandings of these traditions (cf. 1 Cor. 7:25).

Paul then learned of trouble in the Church at Corinth; some were attacking Paul viciously. He made a trip to see them and after his visit to the church, where he was treated rather rudely, Paul left and wrote to them a "painful" or "severe" letter (cf. 2 Cor. 2:1f.). This accomplished the purpose intended by the visit. The Corinthians were now ready to accept Paul and his authority. Again this letter has not survived, at least not intact.[2] Paul, when Titus met him in Macedonia to give him the good news that the severe letter had done what Paul in person could not do, wrote 2 Corinthians 1–9, the "thankful" letter, sometimes called the letter of reconciliation. This letter paved the way for a return visit during which he spent the winter of 56–57 with the church there.

The second major problem during this period was that with the "Judaizers." These were persons who were fomenting trouble in the Galatian Churches and attacking Paul in such a manner as to evoke from him a letter written in the heat of intense anger. Paul did not pull any of his punches in Galatians, indicating that those who pervert his Gospel could "go to Hell, twice" (cf. Gal. 1:6–9)! And further he "advised" his enemies that if circumcision is of such value to go castrate themselves (cf. Gal. 5:12)! Paul argued in this letter the great doctrine of the Reformation, namely the concept of "justification by faith." He sounds much like the prophets of old in this letter, arguing that there could be no escape from the evil and sin and death in the world by external rituals; it is only in a new relationship with God that there is hope.

Another letter that seems most appropriately to have been written during this period is the letter to the Philippians. Traditionally it is usually included with the prison correspondence from Rome (ca. 62 A. D.), but there are good reasons for placing it here. Paul applauded the Philippians for "so soon" having sent aid to him.[3] And there is still in this letter a bitter feeling on Paul's part against the Judaizers, which dispute took place during the Ephesian ministry. In 3:2 he says, "Look out for the dogs, look out for the evil-workers, look out for those who mutilate the flesh," and he then proceeds to defend himself and his gospel as he did in Galatians (3:2f.). The major problem with this theory is that Paul is not known *explicitly* to have been imprisoned in Ephesus, and he is definitely in prison at the time of the writing of this letter (cf. 1:12f.). It is commonly agreed, however, that Acts does not "tell all," and from some of Paul's own statements it is very likely that he may have been, in fact, in prison in Ephesus.

The last letter of this period was written when Paul was spending the winter in Corinth. This is, of course, Paul's most famous letter, the Epistle to the Romans. Paul's plan was to return to Jerusalem with the offering from the churches for the saints in Jerusalem (Romans 15:22f.) and then to come to Rome so that he could preach the gospel in Spain. What was he to say to this church? Paul was not very good at small talk; he had not founded the church; and he probably knew very few people in it and little about their problems.

There are those who think that because of these facts that Paul's letter to the Romans is his "systematic theology." To be sure the letter is one of the most systematic of all his writings, but there are too many "theological doctrines" either omitted or briefly mentioned for this letter to be considered a complete theology. If one reads Romans carefully, it becomes clear what basically lies behind the content of the work—Paul's relationships and problems with the churches which he has just experienced. In other words, the Judaizing controversy and the problems of and with the Church at Corinth form the basis for the content of this letter. Paul wrote what was "on his mind," and because of this the letter is still "occasional" though not as pointedly so as with the other correspondence.

When Paul was imprisoned at Rome he is traditionally said to have written four letters, Philemon, Colossians, Ephesians, and Philippians. It has already been indicated that Philippians may come from an earlier time period, and there is a great debate among New Testament scholars as to whether Ephesians was in fact written by Paul. While many of the phrases and words seem to be taken from Colossians (and other letters), it is also true that there is a wide vocabulary difference between Ephesians and the "authentic" Pauline letters. Further there is a subtle difference in several "theological" points: for example, in Ephesians the "Reconciler" is Christ whereas in Paul's (other) letters the Reconciler is God working through Christ. The most telling argument, however, is the style. If one reads Paul's letters, the style is usually choppy with rather short sentences. Ephesians on the other hand is smooth and flowing. Ephesians, therefore, will be included in a later discussion.

This leaves Colossians and Philemon which were written and dispatched at the same time (cf. Col. 4:12f., Philem. 23–24). These letters were most probably written from Rome. Philemon is one of the most delightful and also most serious of all of Paul's letters. It was written for the very purpose of saving a man's life. The runaway slave, Onesimus, had come upon Paul, been converted to the Christian life, but he still belonged legally (and, in that time, morally) to Philemon. To keep Onesimus with him Paul would be breaking the civil law; to send him back would place Onesimus' life on the line. Paul sent him back, but with this short but potent letter pleading for the life of his newly found Christian brother.

There is debate over the letter to the Colossians as to whether Paul actually wrote this epistle since there are some ideas and vocabulary which are not found in other of Paul's letters. But in this case the style is quite similar to Paul's style and the vocabulary may be different because of the nature of the problem. The Church at Colossae was being exposed to certain teachings of questionable validity. Exactly what these teachings were is not known, but as best as can be determined from the text there were two. One seems to have been basically Jewish in its background (cf. Col. 2:16f.), and the other basically Greek (cf. 1:15f.; 2:8f.; 2:20f.), but these do not appear to be neatly separated in the minds of the people nor in Paul's reply.

The basic issue appears to be that the people there (with their basically Greek background) are confused as to exactly where Jesus fits into the *pleroma*. Is he at the top, bottom? If Jesus is one of the "beings" of the *pleroma* structure, should not the other "beings" be worshiped as well? Paul's basic answer was that Jesus is all there is of the *pleroma* (cf. 1:19; 2:9). There are no beings in a labyrinthian maze of the world super-structure. God through Christ has direct contact with the world of humanity.

And as for the trouble with Jewish food laws, feast days, etc., Paul stood firm in his conviction that these were matters which may be followed but are certainly unnecessary and external to the central essence of the Christian life.

Each of Paul's letters had a unique and separate history. Each was written at a particular time, to a particular place, for a particular purpose. And each probably had different kinds of care. Exactly when the collecting of Paul's letters together into a corpus (body) took place or by whom is not known, but a good guess would be sometime after the publication of the book of Acts (ca. 90 A. D.). That the collection was made and arranged not chronologically but by length of writing (except when there was more than one letter, then the two were not separated) seems to be clear. Some letters appear to be lost, others fragmented, and one perhaps misnamed.[4] What is remarkable is that there were so many preserved and in such a condition as to be extremely close to Paul's very words!

Because there are so many and because these letters are all occasional, it is very difficult to arrange Paul's thoughts in a logical, always consistent pattern. But there are certain themes and ideas that do persist, and some of these deserve special attention.

Some Leading Ideas

If one had to define Paul's basic religious viewpoint, it could be done in much the same way as the Old Testament writers. God through a unique action within the historical process has done something for humanity that it could not do for itself. The historical event is very important, but the meaning of the event is "revelation." Where Paul differs is at the point of the interpretation of the events surrounding Jesus of Nazareth. Through the life-death-resurrection of Jesus, Paul believes, God has somehow removed sin, established life, overcome the forces of evil, and inaugurated a new age.

Books have been written, scholars have argued, and theologians have struggled with what Christianity meant to Paul. Many viewpoints have been expressed, but in spite of all the technicalities and opinions one idea seems to stand out in every letter of Paul's—the idea of the *new life*. Religiously speaking, this is the most important concept in Paul's letters! This new life is available to all persons no matter what their status, and it is a life which is different from ordinary or "normal" human existence. Human beings, according to Paul, are enmeshed in an ocean of sin from which they cannot extricate themselves. This sin is both *inborn* since all are descendants of Adam and *learned* from the environment. Sin is both an inward weakness or even active predisposition toward evil and a force outside of humanity which invades the human life and takes control. It is, in short, a force which has humanity in its grasp; and to Paul this grasp has been broken in God's action in Jesus. Exactly what happened or how, he is unable to explain fully. The results are clear to Paul, however, and persons can be convinced of this transforming power only by experiencing it in their own lives—and those who have not experienced it can (or should) see it taking place in the lives of Christians.

This is not to imply that Paul believed that once a person became a Christian, established a new relationship with God, and had the Spirit working within, that such a person could or would sin no more. Paul, as did the apocalyptic writers, believed in the two-age scheme, but Paul's scheme was different. The new age had come and could be experienced now, but the old age had not yet been destroyed. The picture which is usually drawn is that of two circles which overlap somewhat. The Christian lives then in the shaded area.

Because of this overlap there are many problems to be faced in the new life by the person committed to the life of the new age. The old age under the dominion of evil still is active and aggressive, doing its best to draw those in the new age back into the old.

Many commentators miss this essential point about Paul. Entrance into or commitment to the new life does not automatically transform one; it does not transport a person into a different place of existence, only to a different quality. Therefore the Christian life is basically a struggle, a difficult struggle, which must be renewed each day. This explains why so much of Paul's writing is done in the manner of exhortation. Many commentators, for example, insist on reading Romans 5:1 as an indicative, "we have peace," rather than a subjunctive, "let us have peace," as the overwhelming textual evidence attests. This passage is a good one for illustrative purposes at this point. In Romans 3:21–4:25 Paul has set out his own understanding of the new life that is made available to all and how this new life is appropriated by the person involved. To be sure, God has done all that is necessary for the new life to be a possession of any who will accept it. But while it may be appropriated by the person, it must continue to be renewed each day. The text beginning at Romans 5:1 then should read, "having been justified by faith, *let us continue to have* peace with God, . . . and *let us continue to rejoice* in our hope of sharing the glory of God . . . and *let us continue to rejoice* in our sufferings. . . ." (Cf. Romans 5:1–5.)

What are the characteristics of the person who has been given this new life? There are many. The person has been delivered from bondage to sin (cf. Romans 6). This does not mean that a Christian does not or cannot commit acts of sin, but it does mean that the life of a Christian is not characterized by continual, habitual, and gross sinning. There is in Paul a definite belief that a person grows in this new relationship so that the potential for being a better person tomorrow is always the challenge and the promise (cf. Phil. 3:12–16).

Much has been made of Paul's doctrine of justification by faith. This doctrine was at the heart of the Protestant Reformation and has held great sway over much theological thinking since that time. It has also been viewed as the foundation stone of Paul's thought. The traditional interpretation of this idea is that humanity stands before the court of God, guilty of sin, deserving to die. But because of the action of God accomplished in Jesus, God as the Judge pronounces a verdict of "not guilty" and thus acquits the sinner so that the guilt is removed. It is true that Paul does emphasize that God has removed sin and guilt from humanity, but it is difficult to find in Paul any such idea that God renders a verdict of "not guilty." This would be a violation of God's integrity and righteousness.

Paul rather argues that God has forgiven sin and by so doing "covers" the guilt, but it is also true that the new relationship involves great responsibilities, the basic one being that the person is committed totally to the new relationship which not only forgives the sin and removes the guilt but *also transforms the person!* No one deserves to be called a Christian who does not walk according to the Spirit (cf. Gal. 5:16f.)—and this means a changed life.

This new life is characterized by love (cf. Romans 12:9–18; 1 Cor.

13). This love is not a slushy sentimentalism but genuine concern for and commitment to God and others, *in that order!* In fact, one could argue that the basic cornerstone of Paul's ethic is found in 1 Corinthians 8. In this passage the Corinthians have a difference of opinion over whether they can eat meat which has been offered to idols. It was their belief that when the animal was sacrificed the god actually entered the meat, and by consuming the meat the devotee made the god part of his very being. Naturally the devotee could not eat all of an animal brought in, so the priests at these temples sold the remainder of the meat for their economic livelihood. Was it an act of idolatry for a Christian to eat this meat sacrificed to a god? Would that god become a part of the person who eats? Paul's answer was that it is not an act of idolatry since there are no other gods; therefore one can eat this meat and have no fear of violating any religious scruple at all.

But there is something involved that goes beyond the "religious scruples" motif. That concerns the responsibility of the Christian for other people. As with the Old Testament emphasis on the group, the New Testament and Paul teach that a person is not an island but has duties to others. Even though it may not be morally wrong for a person to eat this meat, if by this action someone else is destroyed, the Christian is to abstain from eating.

The Christian ethic is supposedly based on building up, not tearing down. When the Corinthians are quarreling over who has the greatest "gift" to use in the Church, Paul reminds them that great gifts are meaningless unless they are used in accordance with the greater gift of love. "If I speak in the tongues of men and angels, . . . if I have prophetic powers, and understand all mysteries . . . if I have all faith to remove mountains, . . . if I give away all I have, . . . if I martyr myself for the cause, but do not act out of love, it counts for nothing" (1 Cor. 13:1–3, paraphrase)!

The true mark, then, of the Christian is the new life which is characterized by love and therefore by joy. It is a lifestyle that is different from that of this world, this age. It is a lifestyle characterized by walking in the Spirit, ". . . love, joy, peace, patience, kindness, goodness, faithfulness, gentleness, self-control . . ." (Gal. 5:22–23).

Religiously speaking, the new life is the dominant motif in Paul's thought, but religion does need some content and theory on which to base its actions. There are, therefore, several other ideas which need to be mentioned to make the picture a bit more complete. It should by this time go without saying that central to Paul's thinking was the person of Jesus. Without him and his work there would be no new life or new relationship. To Paul Jesus was God's son in a unique way even though he is always careful to emphasize that the human Jesus, no matter how unique, was always subordinate to God the Father.

Included in Paul's writings, however, are the raw materials out of which later developed Christological thinking and speculation grew. The two most important passages are found in Philippians 2:5–11 and in Colossians 1:15–19. The former is probably a pre-Pauline Christian hymn used by Paul to illustrate the point he is attempting to make to the Philippians, namely that they be humble and agree without bitterness for the building up of the Church to reflect the glory of God.

The Colossians passage is probably a Pauline composition which gives a cosmic dimension to Jesus not heretofore seen in his writings. The reason for this is that the Colossians were confused about where Jesus belonged in the *pleroma* structure; they were also confused about whether to worship or give homage to the other figures in the *pleroma* structure (cf. p. 114). Paul indicated to them that Jesus was the head of the *pleroma;* in fact, there really was no *pleroma* since all the fulness of God dwelt in Jesus bodily. There were no other beings that demanded worship except God and God's own chosen instrument in creation, namely his Christ. And Paul identifies God's Christ with Jesus. It is necessary to remember that these passages were not written nor intended as "theology" *per se* but as answers to questions and problems in the life of the churches. Having understood this, however, it is still abundantly clear that Paul had a very high opinion of the uniqueness of Jesus as God's Son.

Jesus' death also has deep significance for Paul. Even though he is unable to understand the depths of meaning in this action of God, Paul affirms that something unique happened on the cross. While most theologians have emphasized the sacrificial nature of the death as substitution or satisfaction of some sort, Paul himself did not emphasize substitution or satisfaction even though he recognizes that in some way "Christ died for the ungodly" (cf. Romans 5:6). What Paul saw most clearly in the death of Jesus was the way by which God *reconciles* the human race to himself. Out of the background of his own experience with the Corinthian Church he understood better what reconciliation is. When a relationship is broken, it must be restored. When one person is alienated from another and refuses to be reconciled, it is that person (or group) for which something must be done. It is not God's honor or sense of justice or feelings that must be satisfied; it is man's alienation from God and his refusal to return that must be dealt with. In short, the act of God in Jesus on the cross was not done for God's benefit but for humanity's. That this involves forgiveness of sins was obvious as well, for Paul wrote to the Corinthians: ". . . God was in Christ reconciling the world to himself, not counting their trespasses against them, and entrusting to us the message of reconciliation. So we are ambassadors for Christ, God making his appeal through us" (2 Cor. 5:19–20a). The person who accepts this action of God must accept also certain responsibilities among which is the command to share this new life.

The term "Faith" played a large part in Paul's thinking, perhaps not as much as some commentators have believed, however. "Faith" in Paul's writings did not refer to a content of doctrine or belief, but can be understood best in the Old Testament sense of faithfulness or trust. It is again the idea of relationship. One entered into the new relationship with God through trust. This trust was similar to the trust which Abraham had exhibited many years before, a basic trust in the essential righteousness of God, and a response and commitment to God's call. This "election" motif was quite prominent in Paul's life and teaching as well. He felt that all Christians were called or elected to do the same thing that Abraham was elected to do—make this God known in all the earth (cf. Romans 9; 2 Cor. 5:16–21; Gal. 3:28–29).

Paul believed that God's righteousness formed the basis for God's relationship with the world, and that righteousness insured that God would always act in accordance with his own character. He is not arbitrary or capricious but is characterized by love and righteousness in his relationship with all people.

The Pauline teaching on eschatology is much debated. Paul took over from the early Church its proclamation of the kerygma with the emphasis upon Jesus' imminent return. His earlier letters to the Thessalonian Church reflected the belief that it was thought to be unusual for anyone to die before the Parousia. Paul's view there tended to agree with a literalistic apocalyptic interpretation, where persecution preceded God's intervention on behalf of his people (cf. 2 Thess. 2:1–12; 1 Cor. 7:26). There are those who find in Paul, however, a growing awareness that he himself may die before the Parousia (cf. 2 Cor. 5:1f.), and, therefore, there is a shift in emphasis from the apocalyptic, external, literal type of eschatological thinking to a non-apocalyptic, internal, figurative or spiritual type of thinking. Some even argue that Paul completely gave up the idea of a Parousia,[5] but there is little evidence of this in the letters. What he did, however, was to talk more about the believer's fate at the time of physical death (a shift of emphasis), since it had become obvious to him that the Parousia had not come and may be delayed even longer! One is reminded of his discussion in 1 Corinthians 15:35f. and also statements in Philippians 1:23 and 2 Corinthians 4:16f. In these passages he seems to be arguing for a non-interrupted relationship with God that is not broken by physical death. This shift in the priority in his thinking is also evident in his advice to the people in Colossae about everyday life (cf. Col. 3:18–4:6), when compared to his advice in 1 Corinthians 7:25f. where he gave his opinion that, since the Parousia was so close, it would be better not marry. Marriage brings children, and one does not want children to undergo the extreme hardships and sufferings connected with the time of the end of the age. Therefore Paul may very well have shifted his emphasis and obviously thought that the Parousia had been delayed, but there is no evidence that Paul ever gave up this idea. And this is not surprising since it was part of the tradition of the early Church which Paul accepted as going back to Jesus himself!

There are many other themes and ideas of Paul, all of which cannot be examined in a work of this nature. There are, however, several terms which need brief explanation since so many misconceptions are prevalent about them and since Paul used them so often. When examining Paul's use of certain terms, one must remember that he felt perfectly free to use the same term in various ways. Exactly how was determined by the context of his writing. The definitions given here are those for the usual meaning he ordinarily employed when using these particular terms.

One of these words is *flesh (sarx)*. The term in Greek can mean flesh in the sense of physical substance, and it has this meaning in Paul's writings occasionally. Usually, however, the term indicated humankind in the position of being apart from God, in an unredeemed state. He spoke frequently about living (or walking) *according to the flesh*, meaning living a life characterized by the things of the flesh. That this does not mean that *flesh* is in and of itself sinful is probably best illustrated by his enunciation that "the works of the flesh are plain: immorality, impurity, licentiousness, idolatry, sorcery, enmity, strife, jealousy, anger, selfishness, dissension, party spirit, envy, drunkenness, carousing, and the like" (Gal. 5:19b–20). Most of the sins here are "spiritual" or arise from an "evil spiritual disposition." Thus "flesh" in Paul refers most often to humanity in its fallen, unredeemed state, separated from God.

Flesh could also indicate weakness. This is not to be equated with the old Greek idea that "flesh is evil," but Paul believed as some of the Old Testament writers that the flesh as flesh is weak. Because humankind is weak, sin finds opportunity in the flesh to work its evil ways, and this could occur even within a Christian (cf. Romans 7:13–25).

A second term that needs to be defined is the term *body (soma)*. Again this word has various nuances, but one of the chief usages in Paul's thought is that the term refers to the *whole person*. In Old Testament thought the basic essence of the human personality was that a human being was a *psycho-physical* totality, a whole unified person. While there may be parts, i.e., spiritual and physical, these could be separated only to talk about them. So too with Paul. The human being is a holistic totality. There may be heart, mind, life-principle (usually translated wrongly *soul*), body, etc., but each of these in essence refers to the *whole* person. And when Paul and the other New Testament writers talk about salvation, they mean the salvation of the *whole* person, not simply bits and pieces. This is why, when Paul attempted to define the resurrection of the body, he meant much more than the physical resuscitation of a dead corpse. This concept included the living on of the "whole" person, the essence of the personality, in another type of "body" suited for existence in a different, i.e., spiritual, realm (cf. 1 Cor. 15:35–50).[6]

There is one further term which deserves consideration, law *(nomos)*. One must remember when reading Paul that in at least two of his letters the primary focus is upon attempting to demonstrate that salvation cannot be connected in any way with the law. This concept, that of salvation being earned through the keeping of the law, was being espoused by the Judaizers, but the same attitude and thought pattern may have permeated the churches and have been related to specific items other than the law. As for the meaning of the term in Paul's writing, there are places where the term means "principle"; others where it seems to refer to the whole written Torah; and others where Paul seems to separate the ceremonial law from the ethical demands of the law.

In most instances, however, Paul referred generally to the Torah, which would include both ceremonial and ethical requirements, although Paul was always quick to point out that keeping the law does not give new life. For one reason, no one is able to keep the law perfectly (cf. Gal. 5:3) and even if one could, this would not be "religion" but only external form (cf. Phil. 3:4–11). The law is a code written on stone; the new life is a transformed person with the "Law" written on the heart (cf. Romans 7:6).[7]

The Law is a positive good given to humanity by God as a gift to assist persons in their relationship with him, but because of human sin this purpose had become twisted and distorted. Instead of being a guideline or a challenge it became an idol. Instead of being a reflection of the will of God, it became a talisman for human security. According to Paul the law is *still* valid for the purposes it was originally intended to fulfill. The attitude of people toward it must change, because the law *cannot* (and was not intended to) redeem (cf. Romans 7:7–25). The *intention* of the law is important, not the letter! The intention of the law was to serve as a guideline in directing a person already in the proper relationship with God toward love of God and love of one's neighbors.

The law as an external set of directives could never accomplish a transformation of the person or group. That could be done only by the activity of God himself dwelling within, forming a relationship with the believer which changed that person from a self-centered to a God-centered being. In such a circumstance the emphasis fell not on external regulations but on an inner quality characterized by the same kind of love that had been exemplified through the gift of God to humanity, namely Jesus. This love, therefore, should be the distinguishing characteristic of the Christian's new life. And this love insured that the law would be kept at the level at which it was originally intended. "Therefore love is the fulfilling of the law" (cf. Romans 12:8–10).

This leads to one of the most distinguishing of Paul's phrases, "in Christ." As usual with Paul, the term was used in various ways, but there is definitely a usage of the term which is generally designated "mystical." Paul spoke of the relationship of the believer with Christ as being so intimate that the believer is "in Christ." In Paul this mysticism was relational, but too often mysticism is interpreted as "absorption," wherein the believer is absorbed into the deity and loses consciousness and individuality. Not so in Paul, for his concept was that of a "reacting" mysticism not an "acting" mysticism.[8] In other words, the Christian becomes one with Christ because that person has "reacted" to the act of God in Jesus. The believer, therefore, enters into a "mystical" relationship with God "in Christ," but this relationship enhances the individuality of the person rather than absorbing and diffusing that individuality into a greater anonymous and amorphous mass.

There is another dimension to being "in Christ" that is often overlooked. While it is true that the Old Testament emphasizes the group, it is not true that the individual counts for nothing. While it is true that much of the emphasis in the New Testament seems to deal with individuals, it is not true that the group is unimportant. The fact is that the group is perhaps just as important in the New Testament as in the Old. The term "in Christ," therefore, has corporate meanings as well as individual. In fact, one of Paul's favorite analogies (of which he uses many) is that of comparing the Church to a human body (cf. 1 Cor. 12:14f.).

In other words the Christian never exists alone. *Because* a believer has a personal relationship with God, that believer has a personal relationship with others as well. Because believers are "in Christ," they constitute the body of Christ. Because the believers have experienced this new relationship with God and with each other, the

Church can witness to the world (the old age) that the new age (which can and should be seen in the lives of believers) has indeed come.

Additional Readings

Bible: 1 & 2 Thessalonians; 1 & 2 Corinthians; Galatians; Romans; Philippians; Colossians

Secondary Material:

Selby, D. J. *Toward the Understanding of St. Paul.* Englewood Cliffs, N. J.: Prentice-Hall, Inc., 1962.

Fitzmyer, J. A. *Pauline Theology: A Brief Sketch.* Englewood Cliffs, N. J.: Prentice-Hall, Inc., 1967.

Bornkamm, G. *Paul.* Trans. by D. M. G. Stalker. New York: Harper & Row, 1971.

Whiteley, D. E. H. *The Theology of St. Paul.* Philadelphia: Fortress Press, 1964.

Baird, William. *Paul's Message and Mission.* Nashville: Abingdon Press, 1960.

Furnish, V. P. *Theology and Ethics in Paul.* Nashville: Abingdon Press, 1968.

Notes Chapter 9

1. The fact that Paul wrote a brief greeting in his own hand at the conclusion of the letters was obviously necessitated by the fact that some persons were writing letters in his name which contradicted Paul's teaching and were misleading the recent converts to the Christian faith (cf. 2 Thessalonians 2:2; 3:17).

2. It may be possible, however, that some of this letter is preserved in 2 Corinthians 10–13, for the tone and content of these chapters are quite different from that of 2 Corinthians 1–9.

3. Furthermore, there are four round trips mentioned in this letter between wherever Paul was and Philippi. A round trip from Philippi to Rome took about 14 weeks of *constant* travel, but a round trip from Philippi to Ephesus took only about 20 to 24 days.

4. Philemon, for example, may have been the Letter from Laodicea; cf. Col. 4:16.

5. Cf. C.H. Dodd, *New Testament Studies* (Manchester: Manchester University Press, 1953); "The Mind of Paul: II," cf. especially pp. 109–18.

6. As with the term *flesh,* Paul in a few instances used *body* in a way as to refer only to physical aspects of it. These meanings should be kept in mind, but it is usually clear from the context of the saying which of the meanings is intended.

7. Cf. the Old Testament prophets Jeremiah and Ezekiel.

8. These terms and the ideas here belong basically to A. Deissmann, *Paul: A Study in Social and Religious History,* trans. W.E. Wilson (New York: Harper & Row, 1957). Harper Torchbook edition (original ed. 1911, rev. 1927), cf. pp. 147–57. For a similar discussion cf. also James S. Stewart, *A Man In Christ* (New York: Harper & Row, n.d.; London: Hodder & Stoughton, Ltd., 1935), pp. 147–203.

10
The Post-Apostolic Period

In many ways the era known as the post-apostolic period in the development of the Christian Church parallels the post-exilic period in Old Testament history. There were many problems internally, and many pressures, even to the point of persecution externally. It was a period of development, trial and error, frustration, apostasy, consolidation, and survival. While this period is variously dated, perhaps the best dates would be 75/80–150 A. D.

Theologically, the thinking about the Person of Jesus, called Christology, was primary in the minds of the writers during this time. It was not enough simply to say as the Synoptics had done (two of them did, in fact, come from this period) that Jesus was the Messiah, the Son of God. What were the fuller implications of that assertion? Matthew's Gospel reflected the beginning of the more exalted teaching with its emphasis on the worship of Jesus even during his earthly ministry. Other questions naturally arose as well. If Jesus were truly God's Son, what does this say about his pre-existence? If he were truly divine, how could he have any contact with created, weak, even evil, matter? These and other problems arose and had to be considered.

During this period also, Gnostic beliefs more and more began to find their way into Christian thought patterns. One heresy which stemmed directly from Gnostic type ideology centered on the Person of Jesus and was called *Docetism* (from the Greek word "to seem"). These docetics believed that the divine part of Jesus was not really connected with the physical Jesus; it only "seemed" or "appeared" to be. There were differing views even among the docetics as to the exact nature of the divine-human relationship in Jesus. To some the divine element came into Jesus at the time of his baptism but left before the crucifixion (because deity could not suffer); to others Jesus "appeared" to have a human body but was in reality only a phantom materially speaking. This problem occupied much of the thinking of the early Church and continued to do so until 451 A. D.[1]

This same type of Gnostic thinking led to extremes in another area, namely the living of the Christian life. There were two basic distortions. One was the belief that, since all the world is evil, the Christian should withdraw from the world insofar as that is possible. This ascetic tendency was quite widespread and became more so later. The most popular of the extremes, however, was the thought that, since the world and its attendant desires are unimportant, the Christian had no obligation to keep any moral demands. "Eat, drink, and be merry," for the flesh does not count! These ideas did not die out slowly.

Another problem not related to Gnostic influence but of great importance concerned the questions raised by the delay in the Parousia. The early Church had fully expected this event to happen within a generation, but it had not occurred. The failure of that cardinal tenant of the kerygma to come to pass, naturally, was an embarrassment to the Church. A generation had come and gone, but no Parousia. Some became discouraged and decided that it was all a hoax. Others struggled with the problem and offered various solutions to meet the situation.

In spite of the problems the Church continued to exist and to grow. Growth is always a painful experience and raises problems which have to be solved or at least resolved. In addition to the theological problems (and sometimes *because* of them), practical matters needed attention also, especially at the point of Church organization which had become a necessity. Heretofore the Church had been loosely administered by a person or group of persons respected by the local congregation. In the light of the fact that the Parousia was imminent, no formal structure was deemed necessary. What organization there was was primarily practical, and one reads in Paul references to deacons, deaconesses, elders, and bishops. There were other important offices listed as well, such as pastors, teachers, prophets, and the like (cf. 1 Cor. 12:27f.; Romans 12:6f.), but most of these offices were "functional" rather than "political." With the growth of the Church and the obvious delay of the Parousia, it became evident that there was needed some kind of "official" structure in order for the Church to be kept orderly in growth and in doctrine.

With the growth of the Church and its spread over most of the Roman Empire, a major issue was unity. How could unity be achieved with such diversity in membership and geography? This question was made even more difficult with the increase in persecution experienced by the Church. An empire-wide persecution of Christians would probably have done much to unify these diverse groups, but the type of persecution which these early Christians were encountering was sporadic and local. The persecution in Rome in the time of Nero did not appear to have spread elsewhere, and there seems to have been no empire-wide persecution of Christians until the time of Decius (ca. 250 A. D.). There is no doubt that these local persecutions were real and vicious, however.[2]

To these varied and difficult problems numerous leaders of the Church of this era directed their writings. Perhaps the first investigation should be of the works sometimes called "Deutero-Pauline." These are writings which claimed to be from Paul, but there are many weighty arguments which seem to militate against such a conclusion.[3] These are Ephesians, the Pastoral Epistles (1 and 2 Timothy and Titus), and the Letter to the Hebrews, even though this particular book does not claim to be from the hand of Paul.

The Letter to the Ephesians was in all probability a circular letter written to a group of churches in a given area (probably the churches in Asia Minor near Ephesus) to argue for unity in the Church. The style of Ephesians, so different from Paul's letters, rises to great heights of emotion and expression. The author argues for the ultimate unity of all creation in God's purpose as revealed in Jesus Christ. All the "loose ends" of the universe come together in Him (cf. Eph. 2:11–22). Because God makes all things adhere together in Christ, there is an appeal for unity in the Church (cf. 4:4–6) and the appeal for right living on the part of those whose task it is to proclaim to the world by word and deed the "unsearchable riches of Christ" (cf. Eph. 4:17–6:9). According to this author, the Christian life is a constant struggle against the forces of evil (cf. 6:10–20), and this struggle may well be for a long time to come!

The author of this marvelous writing appears to challenge the Church because the world needs what the Church has to offer—God's forgiveness and redemption and transforming power. This ministry has been delegated to Christ and his Church. In order to accomplish this goal, the Church must have unity. Unity does not necessarily mean uniformity, but it does presuppose commitment to the same God and to the same goals. And the members of the Church must further have a strong emphasis upon ethical living because the Church *must* be different from the world, not simply in talk but in deed. The same emphasis is seen here which has been seen so often in the course of biblical thought: God's elective purpose to accomplish his will in this world through a people he has called to labor at the task of making his revelation known to all people.

The letters known as the Pastoral Epistles also claim to be from Paul. It is quite possible that genuine fragments of some Pauline letters are incorporated into these writings, but it is highly unlikely that the letters as they now stand were composed by Paul. They reflect a much more developed stage of Church organization, and certain words such as *faith* seem to carry different connotations from the way they were used by Paul.

The basic problem facing the Church in the Pastorals was the problem of false teaching. The exact nature of this false teaching is not known, but it seems to be related in some way to Gnostic thought. The major threat from false teaching was not primarily theoretical, but rather was of a more practical nature. Since the "theology" of the Church at this time was in a state of fluidity, it was no real problem for persons to hold various viewpoints on certain issues. The major problem, however, came when false teaching led to immoral living. When this occurred, the problem of false teaching became exceedingly serious.

To combat these kinds of ideas and actions the Church began to develop a more formal and rigid system of leadership. In the Pastorals, bishops, elders, and deacons are mentioned. These offices were to be held by persons who are "sound in the faith," faith here being essentially "orthodox" in the traditions of the Church which safeguarded the purity of the Church. The tradition was now developing into a body of "doctrine," and the purpose was essentially the same as that in the post-exilic period, survival and purity of the religious group (cf. 1 Tim. 1:5, 19).

It seems clear that the developing organization was leading to a "bishop" or overseer of the local congregation who had been a member of the group of elders but who had risen above them to a position of superiority. Elders were the next highest order, followed by deacons, whose basic function seems to have been handling the financial and related matters of the local church group. Exactly how the development took place is unknown, but that it did and that it did so primarily as a result of the pressures of "false teaching" seems to be certain.

The writing known as "To the Hebrews" is an enigma to New Testament scholars. Who wrote the book, to whom, and from where are all questions that can be, at best, only guessed at. The reason for the composition is much clearer, however. It seems that there were those, probably in the Church at Rome (cf. 13:24), who were falling away from the "faith." Whether this was a result of the delay of the Parousia or because of persecutions or simply apathy (or a combination of all three) is not clear. If one could hazard a guess, it does seem to be connected with a delay (cf. 10:32f.); and the most likely delay would seem to be connected with the consummation of the Kingdom, i.e., the Parousia. There is also an emphasis upon standing firm in the face of opposition and difficulty; this motif is quite prevalent in the famous "roll-call of the faithful" (cf. 11:1–12:11) and may indicate that these persons had experienced some opposition quite recently.

While the author of this work does not completely ignore the two ages concept, so prevalent in Paul's writings, there is a notable lack of emphasis in Hebrews on this subject. What is found is the idea that there are "two levels" roughly corresponding to the "material" and the "spiritual" realms (cf. 8:1f.; 9:23f.; 11:13–16). Believers have already experienced the "other" spiritual level even though they continue to live in this one. The main concern for this author is, then, the problem of persons falling away from the "faith." His chief argument is that this new religion made possible and available through the act of God in Jesus, who was fully identified with humankind (cf. 4:

14–16), was in a sense "final." This new faith has as its goal redemption, forgiveness of sins, and a new life for the believer. But if one falls away, there is no hope! Because, the full revelation of God has now been given in his Son. ". . . How shall we escape if we neglect so great a salvation" (2:3a, paraphrase)?

The basic methodology utilized by this author is to demonstrate that Jesus is "better than." He argues that Jesus is better than angels, the Law, Moses, the old priesthood and the old sacrifices. In so arguing the author exalts Jesus in such a way as to add to the cosmic dimensions already given to him by Paul in Philippians and Colossians. Therefore Christology is growing, this time as the author tries to demonstrate that the delay in the Parousia and the persecution the Christians are suffering are still lesser items than the "real thing"— Jesus Christ!

There is in Hebrews a great deal of terminology and analogy drawn from the sacrificial system of the Old Testament. Because of this many persons are often left cold by this writing (probably best called an "exhortative homily"). Nevertheless, the understanding by the author and his conviction that this new life is worth more than all the struggle and doubt one can imagine place this book as one of the most significant of all the post-apostolic literature.

Even though persecution seems to have been a part of the problem with the intended hearers of the letter to the Hebrews, two books stand out in connection with persecution and suffering—1 Peter and Revelation. The date of 1 Peter is debated, and it is beyond absolute certainty whether the work goes back to Peter the Apostle ca. 64 A. D., or an unknown person writing in the apostle's name from the time of Domitian ca. 95 A. D. or even as late as the time of Trajan ca. 115 A. D. Whatever the date, the situation seems to be one in which Christians were being persecuted by members of society. Even though some interpreters argue that the state is the villain here, there seems to be little evidence of this from the text. It is known, however, from several writings of this period that there was much misunderstanding about what Christians really did and believed. Some even thought that they practiced cannibalism! In this type of suspicious atmosphere it would be easy enough for all sorts of evils to be attributed to a group such as this, and such a group is always subject to being a ready scapegoat for whatever may go wrong, no matter who or what is really responsible.

In the light of this situation the author of 1 Peter urged the people to endure the suffering because at the time of Jesus' "revelation" (1:7) they would be vindicated. He urged them to bear no grudges (cf. 2:1) and to set an example before others that would leave no doubt about the kind of people Christians were (cf. 2:11–3:9). There seems to be no animosity here towards the state since the readers are urged to "honor the emperor." Christians are to live in such a way that the only suffering which they encounter will be unjustified (cf. 4:14–16). In short, the suffering which they experience is analogous to the suffering that Christ endured. And Christians should not really be surprised at this response from the world; they should expect it.

It is interesting to note that the belief in the Parousia was here used to help bolster the spirits of Christians who were experiencing suffering. And suffering was looked upon as a time of testing to make the lives of Christians better, i.e., in the sense of being refined (cf. 1:6–7) and was a "necessary" prerequisite so that the believer could be prepared to enjoy and in a sense to deserve the exaltation which was to follow (cf. 5:6–10).

If, indeed, the letter known as 1 Peter dealt with local and community persecution, the Book of Revelation reflected another situation. This superb example of apocalyptic literature was written during a period in which Christians were being directly persecuted by the state for their refusal to participate in the cult of emperor worship being actively pushed by the Roman Emperor, Domitian. It is clear from the writing that Christians were actually dying because of their religious convictions.

The book itself is typical of the apocalyptic literary genre we have discussed previously in chapter 6. While the typical apocalyptic characteristics are here, the book itself seeks, in addition, to give some answer as to why the devout and innocent must suffer. The answer may not have been satisfying to some, but it was given as a logical outgrowth of the author's understanding of God. More will be said of this later.

Revelation sought to give hope to and encourage the people who were experiencing the ultimate in persecution. The author (who is not pseudonymous in this apocalyptic work, however) based this hope on the greatness and nature of the God who had intervened in history and had been revealed in Jesus Christ. In spite of all appearances to the contrary, he attempted to demonstrate that it is not Rome but God who rules this world, and while evil must be allowed to run its course, its doom is already sealed.

The historical summary (which most apocalyptic works have) in chapters 12–13 reflect the situation. The woman (Israel) bore a son (the Messiah) who was exalted to God's throne. The Devil, leader of the forces of evil, had already been defeated in the highest places and was thrown down to the earth. He then made war on the woman and her offspring (the Church). He did this by granting his power and authority to the sea-beast (the Roman state) which forced the people to worship evil by means of a cultic priesthood (the second beast). The essence of evil and its power is deception!

The author also made use of the popular belief that Nero would rise from the dead. Since Nero had been the first active persecutor of the Christians, it is easy to see how he could be viewed as the epitome of persecution by the state. It is he who was referred to as the head with the mortal wound (13:3) and in the famous number 666 (or as some texts have it, 616, cf. 13:18). Rome and her emperors, the sea-beast (shown also as a great harlot seated upon a beast in ch. 17), have opposed the will of God and have become so corrupt that they must be destroyed.

When this happens, the old age will pass away and a new age will come. This action by God to accomplish that purpose would be completed *soon*. While the Parousia is not really mentioned in this book, it may be that the author did believe that the final defeat of Rome and the establishment of a new age would constitute the Parousia. It is not certain, however, that the Parousia was expected, but only the end of the persecution.

The problem of suffering is raised rather acutely in this work. Why is it that God's people must suffer? Why does God delay in executing his judgment on evil people? The answer to the first query is relatively simple—the Christian suffers because that person belongs to a different order (the life of the new age), while the world remains under the influence of the old order dominated by sin. The answer to the second question can be discerned in the recurring cycles of judgment which are all partial. Evil must be allowed to run its course because the very nature of evil is self-destructive. The purpose in God's delay of the final judgment is to give even these evil people an opportunity to repent (cf. 9:20f.; 16:11). During that time the righteous faithful suffer. It is the price that is paid for the patience and mercy of God. But there does come a time when that patience and mercy end and nothing is left for the wicked but judgment.

The persecution will end. This is the sure hope of the apocalyptic writer. By exactly what means and when are not known. The Christian readers and hearers were admonished to remain faithful, for nothing can take their names from the book of life—nothing, that is, except their own decision to worship the beast. The judgment will surely come and the earth and heaven will be transformed and persons will be able to worship God again (21–22). And for those who have kept the faith even to death, there will be a special reward (cf. 20:4–6).

Unfortunately, the message of the Book of Revelation has been greatly misunderstood, primarily because there has been much confusion concerning what type of literature it is. As stated previously, the apocalyptic writers composed their works to bolster faith on the part of those who are suffering under grievous hardship. The basic message is simple: Keep the faith; do not commit an act(s) of apostasy; and *soon* the persecution will be ended. And while the great hope is that a new and glorious age will accompany this deliverance from persecution, there is always left open the possibility that sin may not be totally eradicated (cf. 21:24–27). Any attempt to make of this book a timetable for the end of the world is to miss the point of this writing entirely.

It has been demonstrated that the basic problems for the members of the Church were primarily caused by external pressures in 1 Peter, Revelation, and probably Hebrews. But there were many other problems precipitated by internal causes in the Church in this period as well. Some of these were problems of conduct, order in the Church, but most especially problems caused by "false" teaching which had led to immorality in the lives of some members.

The Book of James, so spurned by Martin Luther, is a homily which basically deals with ethical conduct. One of the first arguments of this writing is that persons cannot transfer the blame for temptation to God, as many are often known to do. The author placed the cause of evil in the intense desire inherent in each person (in this he parallels Jesus' teaching in Matthew 5:17f.). There are basically three "evils" which the author discusses: (1) a definition of "faith" that tends to reduce a person's responsibility and obligation for one's neighbor; (2) the misuse of the tongue; (3) jealousy and envy among the members of the Church.

The first of these problems is the most well-known because it is often argued that there was some great disagreement between this writer and Paul. Whereas Paul emphasized "faith," this writer emphasized "works." The great probability is that the two were speaking to entirely different situations. Paul in emphasizing faith was addressing a situation in which persons were arguing that certain ceremonial actions were necessary for salvation. James was writing to a group which had obviously defined faith not as a transforming relationship but rather as a formal credo to be intellectually accepted. James argued in much the same manner as Paul that real faith is completed and demonstrated by "works." Intellectual agreement about doctrine may be fine, but ". . . even the demons believe—and tremble" (2:19b). There had to be more to the Christian life than correct intellectual doctrine.

Another problem was the use or misuse of the tongue. Obviously this had become a major problem in the church James was addressing since he made so much of it, but there is little evidence to indicate exactly what kind of problem existed. Suffice it to say that James approaches the idea that if one can control the tongue, one can control one's life (cf. 3:1–5)!

The third problem was that which concerned the church members' jealousy and selfishness. It is possible that this problem lay at the heart of the admonition to bridle the tongue, but this is only a conjecture. What is clear is that these people were jealous of each other, selfish, and quarrelsome (cf. 3:13–4:12). This attitude contributed to the dissension related to wealth in the church. There seems to be a tendency on the part of these people to "cater" to wealth (cf. 2:1–7; 4:13–5:6). In fact, it may have been that many of these persons were people of some substance who had gotten their wealth by deception and cheating of the common worker, and they had, therefore, no sense of obligation to anyone in need (cf. 1:27; 5:4–6). James argued that in the Church wealth, or the lack of it, counted for nothing. All were equal in God's kingdom.

It can be detected in the reading of this homily that the idea of the Parousia had not died out. In fact, the author obviously believed that the time was near (cf. 5:7–9). Suffering is also alluded to but does not appear to be of a sort directly resulting from an organized effort against the Church as a whole (cf. 5:10–13).

In addition to these basic arguments there are several other motifs that are of interest. One concerns confession of sins, and the thought that this may aid in healing the sick (cf. 5:14–16). Another is concerned with the belief of the author that whoever brings back into the Church a person who has wandered away will ". . . save his soul from death and cover a multitude of sins" (5:20b). It is not exactly clear from the grammar of the sentence whose soul it is that is saved, but it does seem to be certain that the action on the part of the person who is the bring*er* will in some way atone for sins. Further, there is the reference to anointing the sick with oil. This was a common practice in that period, for oil was thought to have medicinal effects. The interesting aspect is that these three concepts all developed into significant activities of the Church in later times.

James is wrestling in his time, however, with the basic problem of proper conduct among the Church members. And it is refreshing to read his homily emphasizing that mere belief without positive action is a religious sham, devoid of meaning!

Another author wrestled with internal problems also, the writer of the three Epistles of John. These letters deal primarily with the internal problems of the Church in terms of false teaching, which basically centered in a docetic doctrine which denied that Jesus had actually appeared in the flesh. This Gnostic emphasis had also led to problems in the relationship among the membership of the Church, those being in the "know" obviously scorning those who were not of their mind. Another problem seems to have centered around the argument as to whether a Christian could sin. Some obviously had answered the question in the negative, perhaps assuming once one had the *gnosis* that the person was lifted beyond ordinary methods of accounting. Others perhaps were arguing that they were not perfect, therefore they need not be concerned unduly over sin!

The author who called himself "the Elder" (cf. 2 John 1; 3 John 1) argued as had James and others that doctrine and practice are inseparably connected. In 1 John we read about "antichrist," but contrary to some popular belief, there is not one but many "antichrists"! The meaning of this term was simply anyone who denied that Jesus had come in the flesh (cf. 2:22f.; 4:1f.).

The problem over sin in the Christian's life appears at first reading to have contradictory answers. The reader was reminded that no one is free from sin and whoever claims to be otherwise is a liar (cf. 1:8–10). Later the author told his people that no one who "abides" in God sins (cf. 3:4f.). The usual explanation of this "contradiction" is that the first statement was directed at those who felt that they were above any rules or regulations since they were possessors of *gnosis*. It is a not so gentle reminder that no one can escape acts of sin. The second statement is directed at those who felt that moral principles were no longer binding on a Christian since the "flesh" does not really count for anything. These people were reminded that those who abide in God do not sin; the tense of the Greek verb here indicates that the person abiding "in God" is not able to live a life that is characterized by constant, continual, and gross sinning. In other words, no Christian can escape doing certain acts of sin, but no Christian can live a life characterized by habitual and gross sinning.

The members of the Church were reminded that love was to be the characteristic feature of their lives, especially in their relationships with one another. "Perfect love casts out fear. . . . We love, because he first loved us. If any one says, 'I love God,' and hates his brother, he is a liar . . ." (1 John 4:18–20).

There was, therefore, a growing tendency reflected in the works of this period and certainly echoed in these Johannine Epistles to establish norms and standards by which teaching and living could be measured. There was an ever growing feeling that Christianity had lost its spontaneous gift of the Spirit and enthusiasm which characterized the early Church. Yet even in this different type of atmosphere the foundation had already been laid upon which the Church could rely even when the spontaneity was missing. It is the idea that love can be the glue which holds everything together in good times and bad. Initially, the belief that the Parousia was imminent had been the motivating force in the growth of the Church. But this kind of impetus is only for a short time; something must be established that will serve as the foundation for the "long haul." This something was love—love of God and love of neighbor, and all that these meant.

The latest of the New Testament writings are Jude and 2 Peter. Scholars usually date them late, perhaps as late as 150 A. D. Whether this is correct is not an issue for this study, but it is true that these two books do belong together since 2 Peter made use of Jude (cf. Jude with 2 Peter 2). The Book of Jude deals basically with false teaching, probably of the Gnostic type, which led some persons into immoral living especially in the sexual realm (cf. vv. 4, 7, 10, 12, 15, 16). Their arrogance also caused divisions in the Church community. This Gnostic type false teaching led the author to view "faith" as the accepted authoritative body of tradition which had been passed down from the beginning of the movement (v. 3). It must be emphasized, however, that the quarrel is not so much with diverse teaching ideas as it is with the immoral living patterns that are direct outgrowths of the perverted teaching.

The pseudonymous author of 2 Peter faced much the same type of situation as the author of Jude. In fact, he incorporated much of Jude into his own work. The new element which this writer discussed was the question about the delay of the Parousia. By this time many had simply given up on the idea. They asked, "Where is the promise of his coming? For ever since the fathers fell asleep, all things have continued as they were from the beginning of creation" (3:4). This author met these questions by arguing that God does not count time as humans do, and that a short time to God may well be a long period as humanity experiences it. He reaffirmed his own basic conviction that there would be an end with fire "dissolving the elements" (3:10), and new heavens and a new earth established in which righteousness would dwell (3:13).

There is one further aspect of this book which deserves mention. The author refers to Paul's letters as "scripture" (3:15–16), which indicates the lateness of the writing but also that Paul's letters had been collected, probably with some other literature, and that these writings were considered authoritative.

This period of the Church's history was one of trial and struggle. The Parousia had not come. The apostles were dead (with the possible exception of John), and the Church's growth necessitated some sort of administrative organization. What kind of conduct was acceptable, and what constituted legitimate teaching, and how one distinguished between the true and false teachings were just some of the problems confronted by this new movement. How were these people to interpret and how were they to react to the types of persecution they were experiencing? In the light of the fact that the Parousia had been delayed, what should be the foundation upon which the Church could build for the future? All these questions and more were weighing heavily on the Christian people in this stage of the Church's development. These writers in the post-apostolic period attempted to deal with the problems by reinterpreting the traditions of the earliest times. Perhaps the most brilliant of all the attempts at reinterpreting the traditions of the early Church was accomplished by the author of the Fourth Gospel.

Additional Readings

Bible: Ephesians; 1 Timothy; Hebrews; Revelation; 1 Peter; James; 1 John

Secondary Material:

Goguel, Maurice. *The Primitive Church.* New York: Macmillan Co., 1964.

Lietzmann, Hans. *The Beginnings of the Christian Church.* Trans. by B. L. Woolf. New York: Charles Scribner's Sons, 1937.

Caird, G. B. *The Revelation of St. John the Divine.* Harper's New Testament Commentary Series. New York: Harper & Row, 1966.

Beckwith, I. T. *The Apocalypse of John.* Grand Rapids, Michigan: Baker Book House, 1967. (Reprint of original edition of 1919.) Old but still excellent on the apocalyptic literature and the book of Revelation.

Beasley-Murray, G. R. *The Revelation of John.* The New Century Bible Series. Greenwood, S. C.: The Attic Press, 1976.

Notes Chapter 10

1. It was in 451 A.D. that the Council of Chalcedon "finally" agreed on what has been accepted as "orthodox Christology."

2. Cf. for example the correspondence between the Emperor Trajan and Pliny the Younger, ca. 112 A.D. For an excellent presentation of these letters cf. J.L. Price, *Interpreting the New Testament* (New York: Holt, Rinehart and Winston, Inc., 1971), 2nd ed., pp. 479–80.

3. It was not considered a matter of immorality or illegality in those days to write a work and attribute it to someone else. There were various factors at work in such a procedure, however. The first is that of honoring the one in whose name the writing was made. It was further thought that writing in the name of a person considered to be an authority or worthy of respect would command more respect for the contents of the writing which presumably would be what that person would say if he were here! Finally, there was the specific intention on the part of the writer to help those people to whom and for whom he wrote.

11
The Gospel of John

Each of the New Testament writings is an interpretation of the "Christ-event," the life and ministry of Jesus and its meaning. And, as has become clear with an investigation of the New Testament literature, most of these writings by necessity reinterpret the tradition because of new and pressing circumstances in the *Sitz im Leben* (setting in life) of the early Church. There is, however, perhaps no greater interpretation than that found in the Fourth Gospel, for it is here that significant "advances" in the areas of Christology, ecclesiology, and eschatology may be found.

Even though the Fourth Gospel was late in appearing, it claims at several points "eyewitness" validity. In some way the traditions preserved here are believed to have gone back to the Apostle John. Whether John himself wrote the Gospel or whether it was a "Johannine school" which produced this work (and the Epistles) is not a concern for this discussion. What is of importance is the fact that there is here a "new" Gospel which does not follow the Synoptic outline or tradition. Written probably during the last decade of the first century A. D., this Gospel reflects the mature thinking of someone who had meditated in some depth on the meaning of all these happenings.

There are numerous ways in which the Gospel of John differs from the Synoptics. One obvious point is that of chronology and location. In the Synoptics Jesus' ministry lasted only from six to eighteen months and was centered in Galilee until he finally went to Jerusalem where the crucifixion occurred. In the Fourth Gospel the ministry lasted from two to three years (possibly even three to four) and included numerous trips to Jerusalem. For example, in the Synoptics Jesus taught in parables and wisdom sayings, whereas in John he spoke in long involved discourses. In the Synoptics the central message of Jesus' teaching was the Kingdom of God, cloaked in apocalyptic terminology, but in John the Kingdom of God was mentioned only once or twice and had been replaced by the term "eternal life." In two of the Synoptics, Mark and Luke, there was a secrecy motif as to Jesus' exact identity, but in John he was recognized almost immediately by some as God's Messiah, the King of Israel. In the Synoptics the eschatological teachings were fairly evenly divided between the present and the future, but in John with few exceptions the emphasis was upon the present. The one who believes in Jesus *has* eternal life (cf. 5:24). Whereas in the Synoptics the eschatological emphasis is upon the two ages concept, a basically linear motif, in John the emphasis is upon a two-level concept, with the primary focus being here upon the upper level. The upper level is parallel to the lower level, and both are included within the historical process. And both are heading toward a conclusion, the linear idea not being entirely gone. The thrust of John's teaching, however, centers on the *level* of one's existence. Is one "from above" or "from below"?

In the Synoptics events happened to Jesus over which he had little control; in John nothing happened except as he allowed it to transpire! In the Synoptic Gospels Jesus, while seen as God's Son and Messiah, was nevertheless human—hungry, angry, frustrated, amazed. The Johannine Jesus did not appear to be a part of the human sphere even though the author continually emphasized his humanity. Jesus usually showed no emotion except anger or perhaps contemptuous amazement at persons who did not understand his message and mission, and who attempted to force his hand to accomplish his task in a way not acceptable to him (cf. 2:4; 7:6; 11:33f.). In the Synoptics the mighty works of Jesus, i.e., the miracles, were illustrations to demonstrate that the Kingdom of God had indeed broken in upon humanity. In John the miracles were called "signs" and interpreted in much the same way as the old prophetic signs. These acts had, therefore, a much deeper meaning and were themselves part of the accomplishing of the goal of the message. There are, then, significant differences between the Synoptic portrait of Jesus and the Johannine portrait.

This consideration necessitates an examination of the basic methodology used by the author in the painting of his portrait of Jesus. The book appears to be consciously written on two levels. The first and most obvious is the literal level. For example, Jesus changed water into wine (2:1–11), but the second deeper or "spiritual" level contains the message the author wished the readers to comprehend. Jesus is not simply a miracle worker but, wine being a symbol of life, the One who can give *real* life. In addition, one of the most usual ways in which the author would introduce a long discourse by Jesus was to depict a scene in which Jesus, having made a statement which was understood almost grossly literalistically, took the opportunity to embark on a long discourse to explain what he really wanted understood. For example, the word used in the dialogue with Nicodemus which Nicodemus interpreted to mean literally "again" (3:3) can mean either "again" or "from above" in the Greek. Since Nicodemus interpreted the saying literally in an almost crude way, Jesus had the opportunity to talk about what being born of the Spirit is all about (cf. 3:5f.). In the discussion with the woman at the well (ch. 4), Jesus told her that if she would drink "living" water which he would give to her she would never thirst again. She wanted to know how Jesus was going to get the water since he had no bucket or rope and the well was deep, but she wanted the water so that she would not have to come to the well and crank it anymore! This pattern of misunderstanding and explanation is continued throughout the entire book.

Even though there are many similarities between the Synoptics and John, there are many differences, sometimes in subject matter, sometimes in emphasis and meaning between the subject matter common to both. For example, the story of the feeding of the 5,000 is in the Synoptics a miracle story to illustrate the fact that the Messiah was able to prepare a feast in the eschatological Kingdom. In John the feeding became the vehicle for Jesus' discourse on being the Bread of Life who dispenses real life through a "mystical" union of the believer with himself.

When one turns to the Johannine Christology, several matters seem to stand out. The Fourth Evangelist has emphasized Jesus' sonship with God quite explicitly and forcefully. This is done at the

very beginning with the famous Prologue (1:1–18) which is a poem
or hymn to the "Word." In the Greek the term which is used is *logos,*
which can mean "word," "reason." This term was used both in Judaism and in Hellenism in somewhat technical ways. In Judaism it could
refer to the Old Testament "word" of God or to something like
"wisdom" personified. In Hellenism the Stoics had a doctrine of the
"logos" as the ordering principle of the world. It was also used in the
Hermetic literature, a gnostic group of writings which reflects some
of the thinking of this type about the time of John's Gospel. Even the
great Jewish philosopher Philo had made use of the idea as he attempted to blend Judaism and Greek thought. Scholars argue concerning which of the background motifs is foremost in John's mind,
but it is perhaps best to judge the *Logos* doctrine in the Gospel by
what the author made of it rather than by what the background was.
Suffice it to say that it was a well known concept both among Jews
and Greeks and was utilized because of that familiarity.

The prologue sets the stage for the entire Gospel. It introduces the
readers to the One who would be the central figure in the story which
followed, and it identifies the historical Jesus with the eternal *Logos*
of God. This hymn goes beyond Paul and the author of Hebrews and
the Synoptic writers in pushing back the origin of Jesus' spiritual
nature. He is not simply a priest forever as in Hebrews, the Son of God
as in the Synoptics, the first born of all creation or the "emptied"
servant of Paul (cf. Colossians 1 and Philippians 2), but the identification is pushed all the way back to God and the "beginning." "In the
beginning was the *Logos,* and the *Logos* was with God, and the *Logos*
was God" (1:1). It is interesting to note that the last clause of the verse
emphasizes "God," not the *Logos.* This can be determined by an
examination of the Greek syntax. Therefore, the author argues that
God and the *Logos,* while separate, are identical! And he further
states that the *Logos* became a human being and dwelt among other
human beings (cf. 1:14).[1] The purpose was to dispense *real* life and
to reveal the very essence of God.

The *Logos* motif for all its background in Hellenism and Judaism
must be viewed against its place in the Gospel. The two motifs already
mentioned are established at the very beginning and continue
throughout the work, namely the creative aspect and the revelatory

aspect of God's Son. These are constantly reiterated as Life and Light. In John the *Logos* is the dispenser of true life, real, genuine, authentic life. As light it dispels darkness, not only by revealing what God was like, but also by shining upon the world and making it impossible for people to argue that they were ignorant of what the world or what each individual was really like. These two themes of Life and Light, Creation and Revelation, are interwoven into the warp and woof of the Gospel story, and they reflect the essential facets of the *Logos* become flesh. It is also interesting to note that after the Prologue the term *Logos* is not mentioned again, for to this author Jesus of Nazareth *is* the *Logos.*

As for the concept of the Church in John, there is a marked emphasis upon the individual and the spiritual nature of the relationship between a believer and God, but the individual is nevertheless a part of the Church since there is no concept of a group of individuals living separate lives apart from one another. The Church is basically conceived as a *fellowship* of persons who had received the new life from the *Logos* and who are bound together by the new commandment—love (cf. ch. 13).

Eschatology has been redirected as well. The older idea of the two ages had given way to the idea of the two levels of existence. In fact some scholars feel that the Parousia has been totally reinterpreted, "spiritualized" and individualized in 14:1–3. In that passage the emphasis centers on the individual's death and that Jesus' "coming" or Parousia was his Presence with the believer especially at the time of the believer's death.

Perhaps the most effective way to interpret the Gospel is to summarize its contents. After the Prologue which introduces the entire Gospel, there are the traditional scenes with John the Baptist and the call of the disciples. But in this Gospel John does *not* baptize Jesus; he only sees the Spirit descend on him. The disciples recognize immediately that this was the Messiah. Chapters 2–12 form the first major section which has been called the "Book of Signs." And the section begins with the pericope of the wedding at Cana, the point of which is that the old Jewish religion (symbolized by the water in the jars for purification) has been superseded by the new life dispensed by the *Logos,* symbolized by the wine of the best quality. Further, this episode is immediately followed by the cleansing of the Temple (at the very beginning of Jesus' ministry in John), the point of which is that there is a new place of worship. No longer is worship restricted to the physical building; it centers in the resurrected body of the *Logos* which is unlimited by time or space or geographical locale. For those who are "in Him" there is no place of worship only a state of worship. One's entire life is to be an act of worship.

The next few chapters are directed toward the concepts of eternal life. The episode with Nicodemus speaks about the birth "from above" (by the Spirit). The episode with the woman of Samaria concerns what authentic worship was all about. The fifth chapter enters into a discussion of who the *real* Son is and that it is he who dispenses eternal life. The discourse on the Bread of Life (ch. 6) centers on the new relationship that is established between a believer and the *Logos,* a relationship so close and so intimate that it can only be described by the metaphor of eating the flesh and drinking the blood of the Son of Man. In chapter seven Jesus goes up to the feast of Tabernacles (Booths) and proclaims that he is the one who dispenses living water (7:37f.). At the same time he gave a discourse on being the light of the world (8:12f.) which led to a debate with the religious leaders which culminated in the famous saying, "Before Abraham was, I am" (8:58b).

After giving the discourse on being the Light of the World, Jesus then proceeds to heal a man born blind (ch. 9), who later comes to believe that Jesus is the "Son of Man." It is interesting that throughout the Gospel the author continues to plead for faith that was based upon the inward experience, *not upon external acts or circumstances.* And the man born blind does *not* believe because of the healing but only later after he comes to understand the meaning and essence of the Person who had healed him. In chapter ten Jesus gives a discourse on his being the Good Shepherd who knows the sheep by name and who lays down his life for the sheep. In chapter eleven, the focal point of the first section of the Gospel, Jesus raises Lazarus from the dead to illustrate that he was indeed the true dispenser of life. He calls Lazarus by name to come out of the tomb, and this action is the trigger that causes the Sanhedrin to decide that Jesus must die.

It is in chapter twelve that Jesus is visited by the Greeks, and when this occurs he says, "The hour has come for the Son of man to be glorified" (12:23). This illustrates two points: (1) throughout the Gospel persons had continually tried to force his hand, urging him to do things that would call attention to himself and precipitate the ultimate intervention of God. He had argued that this was not the way to accomplish the purpose of God, and each time made the statement that "My hour has not yet come." Now it is here. (2) Further, it had been the emphasis of the author that Jesus' glorification was to center not simply in the resurrection, as important as that was, but the glorification of the Son of Man was to take place on the cross. To the author the cross was the throne of the *Logos!*

There is an interlude now between the hectic public ministry of Jesus (the Book of Signs) and the Passion narrative (chs. 18–20). These chapters are usually called the "Farewell Discourses" (13–17). It is interesting to note that the meal eaten together in the Fourth Gospel was a fellowship meal on the *eve* of the Passover, not a Passover meal as in the Synoptics. And it is interesting to note further that the emphasis here was not upon the meal but the teaching attached thereto. This process begins with Jesus' performing the act of a common servant or slave by washing the feet of the disciples, and by indicating to the disciples that this was the manner a person would enter and participate in the Christian fellowship—by performing menial tasks for others in the fellowship. And after Judas, the betrayer, leaves, Jesus then can give a new commandment by which all persons everywhere would recognize these followers of the *Logos.* "A new commandment I give to you, that you love one another; even as I have loved you, that you also love one another." (13:34)

He further instructed them with the teaching about "coming" to them (14:1f.). He argued that he was the true revelation of God (14:8f.), and he indicated that by his departure the Spirit would be given to them. This entity, the Spirit, was given a name in this Gospel, the *Paraclete.* The basic function of the Paraclete was to teach them all things (14:26) and guide them into all the truth (16:13). The idea of growth and development is quite clear here, indicating perhaps that the author had given up on any quick return (perhaps on any return) as the earliest Christians had interpreted it.

There is a call also for patience and stamina in the face of persecution, indicating that the author expected Christians to face difficult roads ahead and for a long period of time (16:31–33).

The section concludes with a long prayer of Jesus, sometimes called the "High Priestly" prayer (ch. 17). In it Jesus defines eternal life as a relationship (17:3) and speaks about the Church in the world. He adds a special prayer for those who would hear and believe because of the testimony of the apostles, and he adds that they should be unified through their intimate relationship with God and himself (17:20–26).

Chapters 18–20 contain the Passion narrative, which is similar to the Synoptic account but interspersed with Johannine emphases. The soldiers are not able to take Jesus until he allows them to do so (18:1f.). The conversation before Pilate depicts the latter puzzled over what "truth" had to do with this trial (18:38). Further, Jesus is slain at exactly the same time the Passover lambs are being slaughtered (19:14f.).[2]

The twentieth chapter is, of course, the climax of the Gospel, not so much because it tells about the resurrection in glory—because to John the entire life of Jesus was one of glory and the cross was his throne—but because it culminates in the message the author has been attempting to proclaim throughout the entire Gospel. That message is an urgent plea for people to enter into this new life-giving relationship with the *Logos* freed from any external or material "proofs." Jesus tells Mary in the garden not to keep on clinging to him (i.e., the physical Jesus, cf. 20:11f.), for it is the resurrected Jesus freed from all kinds of material limitations that releases the believer into the sphere of the new life.

The true climax comes, however, in the scene with Thomas, who has not seen the risen Lord and who vigorously protests that he will not believe until he has placed his finger in the nail prints and his hand in the side. Jesus appears and invites Thomas to do exactly what he had wanted, but Thomas then confesses: "My Lord and my God!" (20:28). But this confession is *not* the central point; the central point is contained in Jesus' following statement, "Have you believed because you have seen me? Blessed are those who have not seen and yet believe" (20:29). The appeal for a faith-relationship not based on external "proofs" reaches full force at this point. Faith to the author of the Fourth Gospel, as it was to so many biblical writers, is a relationship that must be experienced, and no amount of external evidence could convince anyone of its validity—not even stupendous miracles! A meaningful relationship with God must be accepted through trusting him and experiencing the transforming power for oneself.

Additional Readings

Bible: John

Secondary Material:

Hunter, A. M. *The Gospel According to John.* The Cambridge Bible Commentary Series. Cambridge: Cambridge University Press, 1965.

Brown, R. E. *The Gospel According to John,* 2 vols. Anchor Bible Series. Garden City, N. Y.: Doubleday & Co., 1966, 1970.

Marsh, John. *The Gospel Of St. John.* The Pelican Gospel Commentaries. Baltimore, Maryland: Penguin Books, 1968.

Smith, D. Moody. *John.* The Proclamation Commentaries Series. Philadelphia: Fortress Press, 1976.

Notes Chapter 11

1. At this point the author of John lost all the Gnostics and Docetics!

2. It is only in this Gospel that the stories about the mother of Jesus being entrusted to the "beloved disciple" and the soldier piercing Jesus' side with the spear (19:31–37) are found.

12
Conclusion

The fundamental purpose of this book has been to describe the development of the basic religious ideas of the Old and New Testaments. There has been very little attempt, deliberately so, to enter into a discussion about the uniqueness of the biblical teachings, or about the problems of inspiration or revelation or authority. Many books have been written on these topics, and it is not the purpose of this volume to enter into a detailed discussion of such matters. (For those who wish to do so the suggested readings at the conclusion of this chapter will give some guidance in these areas.)

It would perhaps be in order, however, to comment briefly on the general idea of "uniqueness" in the biblical tradition, for there are many who are eager to learn just what it is that is original or unique about the religion of the Bible. All too often, however, persons who search for uniqueness are frustrated, for it is exceedingly difficult to pinpoint precisely what is absolutely different in the religious ideas of the Bible from similar ideas or types of approach or teachings found in other religions or philosophies. Some have argued that the uniqueness of the biblical tradition is its emphasis upon the importance of history in the revelatory process, some even calling this biblical "history" "Salvation history"; and there is no denying the importance and centrality of the historical arena in the religion of the biblical writers. But there are other religions and philosophies that take history seriously, too. Some find the key to uniqueness in the idea of the relationship of God with the world and with human beings, but many other religions have emphasized this as well. Some find uniqueness in the

promise-fulfillment approach which sees the Old Testament as basically looking forward to promises to be fulfilled in the events connected with the New Testament; but there are other ideologies which
have a promise-fulfillment motif. Some find the unique factor in the
figure of Jesus as incarnate Son of God and as the one who has risen
from the dead, but incarnational ideas and resurrection motifs are not
unique to Christianity, and "Sons of God" abound in the history of
the religions of this world.

In reality the uniqueness of the religion of the Bible is that is what
it is! The religious teachings of the Bible include elements from many
different customs and times, religions and philosophies, which when
put together do form a unique set of religious ideas. The most
"unique" is in all probability the understanding of God that is ultimately distinctive and peculiar to the biblical witness. Biblical religion
basically and fundamentally revolves around the assumption that it
is God who is revealed—not so much facts *about* God as much as God
himself, his Personality or Personhood, his Being. Whatever else the
Bible does, it witnesses in almost every book to a God who is held in
awe and respect by his devotees, and whose character and personality
are revealed in the interchange between the person of God and the
history and thought of the people who attempted to know and serve
him and to respond as best they could to the revelation made available
to them.

The twin themes of this God's revelation of himself are mystery
and surprise. The greatness and majesty of this God made him other
than humankind, the specifics of his being not accessible to human
intelligence. The only aspects of his being that could be known inher-
ently were that he existed and that he created (cf. Rom 1:18f.). When
he did reveal himself specifically, however, there was always an element of surprise, because he never conformed to the presuppositions
of human thoughts about him nor to human standards of value. He
is throughout depicted as a God who is different.

From the context of a world permeated by various and sundry
beliefs in many gods with different styles, regulations, and requirements, the biblical writers experienced a god who was different.
Shrouded in mystery, hidden from the mind and eye of humankind,
Yahweh nevertheless wished to know and to be known by the world.

As one among many, the god of a nomadic people, a war god, a god who was connected with and limited to the people and land of Palestine, he came to be understood as the God who knows no other god, who is not restricted or limited by his people nor by geography, nor by time or space. He came to be understood as King of Kings and Lord of Lords, subject to no one or no power except himself. In fact one prime factor in the development of the understanding of the revelation of this God was the realization that he cannot be manipulated by human beings. No amount of bribery, magical hocus-pocus, external ritual or the like could be used to win favor before him.

The concept of the kingdom or reign of God came to be understood not as an externalized political entity but rather as a spiritual force which transforms life, turns the world's values upside down, which somehow releases the created order and the human race from bondage to decay and sin, and which envisions a new world in which old standards would be abandoned and in which all persons would be considered important.

There was to be no substitute for a genuine and total commitment of a person's life to this God and his standards. For this commitment one was not promised an easy life, free from care or tragedy, but rather a new way of living which distinguished the people of God from the people of the world. Because the world was different, the people of God would expect to experience the opposition of the world. And further, the believer could not expect to find all the answers to all the problems and questions of this world. Part of the package was for the people of God to remain faithful even in the midst of disorder, lack of understanding, and even persecution.

Another factor in this revelatory process was the figure of Jesus of Nazareth. Not only is the claim made by the people who responded in faith to his appearance that this Jesus was uniquely the "Son of God," but the emphasis is again placed on the idea that this revelation was different. Whereas the people were looking for a warlike Messiah who would eliminate the enemies of God's people with mighty strength, what actually occurred was the sending of a Person who taught that God's kingdom or rule had nothing to do with kingdoms as humanity understood them. The basic teaching here was that God has sent his Messiah who was supposed to be a marauding Lion but who, as it turned out, was a Lamb—and a slain Lamb at that! A crucified Messiah was unthinkable to the Jewish people, an offense, and to the Gentiles it was sheer stupidity. Even in the midst of the highest revelation of God the twin themes of mystery and surprise were still primary.

In other words, God could not be known according to the biblical witness in specific terms unless he revealed himself to persons who would be receptive to that revelation. And when the revelation did come, it was always a surprise in that this God seemed in every way to be different from the world and human thought. Some, even today, see in this revelation of God a unique inspired authority, while others see only another "interesting" example of human religious development. What makes the difference? It is, of course, a faith response. The biblical books always challenge the reader to respond in faith to the revelation of God which is found there and to be committed to the new relationship with God which is made available to humanity for the purpose of giving a new kind of life, a new essence of life, a new way of life to all who will respond and commit themselves to this new relationship. These books were written to inspire faith and to challenge the reader and hearer of their words to accept what the writers had experienced as the Truth. In a sense then the essence of the biblical revelation (as the writers and devotees understood it) and the reason for the writing down of these understandings are summarized in the concluding verses of the Gospel of John (20:30–31): "Now Jesus did many other signs in the presence of his disciples, which are not written in this book; but these are written that you may believe that Jesus is the Christ, the Son of God, and *that believing you may have life in his name.*"

Additional Readings

Smart, James D. *The Interpretation of Scripture.* Philadelphia: Westminster Press, 1961.

————. *The Strange Silence of the Bible in the Church: A Study in Hermeneutics.* Philadelphia: Westminster Press, 1970.

Morris, Leon. *I Believe in Revelation.* Grand Rapids, Michigan: Wm. B. Eerdmans Publishing Co., 1976.

Barr, James. *The Bible in the Modern World.* London: SCM Press, 1973.

Beegle, D. M. *Scripture, Tradition and Infallibility.* Grand Rapids, Michigan: Wm. B. Eerdmans Publishing Co., 1973.

Bibliography

To become a serious student of the Bible, there are certain basic resources which one needs to assist in the process of studying the Bible. The following books are recommended from a large list of materials available. No attempt is being made here to list all the available sources, not even all the good ones, but the following are especially helpful. The reader is also reminded of the lists cited at the conclusion of each chapter of the text for additional works of value.

Bible Atlases:

Oxford Bible Atlas. H. G. May, ed. New York: Oxford University Press, 1962.

The Westminster Historical Atlas to the Bible. Revised edition. G. E. Wright and F. V. Filson, editors. Philadelphia: Westminster Press, 1956.

Bible Dictionaries:

Dictionary of the Bible. James Hastings, editor. Revised edition by F. C. Grant and H. H. Rowley. New York: Charles Scribner's Sons, 1963.

Interpreter's Dictionary of the Bible. G. A. Buttrick et al., editors. 4 Volumes. New York: Abingdon Press, 1962. *Supplementary Volume,* 1976.

One-Volume Bible Commentaries:

Interpreters One Volume Commentary on the Bible. Charles M. Laymon, ed. Nashville: Abingdon Press, 1971.

The Jerome Biblical Commentary. R. E. Brown, J. A. Fitzmyer, and R. E. Murphy, editors. Englewood Cliffs, New Jersey: Prentice-Hall, Inc., 1968.

Peake's Commentary on the Bible. Revised edition. M. Black and H. H. Rowley, editors. New York: Thomas Nelson & Sons, 1962.

Books Dealing with the History of the Periods:

Bright, John. *A History of Israel.* Second edition. Philadelphia: Westminster Press, 1972.

Bruce, F. F. *New Testament History.* Revised edition. London: Oliphants, 1971.

Historical-Critical Introductions to the Old and/or New Testament:

Anderson, B. W. *Understanding the Old Testament.* Third edition. Englewood Cliffs, New Jersey: Prentice-Hall, Inc., 1975.

Gottwald, N. *A Light to the Nations.* New York: Harper & Brothers, 1959.

Davies, W. D. *Invitation to the New Testament.* Garden City, New York: Doubleday & Co., 1966.

Kee, H. C., F. W. Young, and K. Froelich. *Understanding the New Testament.* Third edition. Englewood Cliffs, New Jersey: Prentice-Hall, Inc., 1973.

Price, J. L. *Interpreting the New Testament.* Second edition. New York: Holt, Rinehart, and Winston, Inc., 1971.

Spivey, R., and D. M. Smith. *Anatomy of the New Testament.* Second edition. New York: Macmillan Co., 1974.

Introductions to the Bible:

Flanders, H. J., Jr., and B. C. Cresson. *Introduction to the Bible.* New York: Ronald Press, 1973.

Fowler, George P. *Our Religious Heritage: A Guide to the Study of the Bible.* Dubuque, Iowa: Wm. C. Brown Book Co., 1969.

Grelot, Pierre. *Introduction to the Bible.* New York: Herder & Herder, 1967.

Hayes, John H. *Introduction to the Bible.* Philadelphia: Westminster Press, 1971.

Mould, E. W. K. *Essentials of Bible History.* Third revised edition by H. Neil Richardson and R. F. Berkey. New York: Ronald Press, 1966.

Wood, James D. *The Interpretation of the Bible: A Historical Introduction.* London: Gerald Duckworth & Co., Ltd., 1958.

Wright, G. E., and R. H. Fuller. *The Book of the Acts of God.* Garden City, New York: Anchor Books, Doubleday & Co., 1960.